THE COMPLETE GUIDE TO INTERNET MARKETING

FOR AUDIOLOGISTS & HEARING PRACTICES

Ignite Your Practice Growth Online

SHANE GEBHARDS

The Complete Guide to Internet Marketing for Audiologists and Hearing Practices

How to Ignite Your Practice Growth Online

By

Shane Gebhards

Copyright © 2020 Shane Gebhards

All Rights Reserved.

ISBN:

Dedication

This book is dedicated to my beautiful wife, Lauren Gebhards. You are my inspiration and the reason I work so hard. In addition, my true passion in life is helping business owners increase their sales, grow their business and accomplish their goals. I want to thank all the wonderful business and practice owners that have allowed me to hone my craft by working with their business. You know who you are and I could not have written this book without the real world experience that your company afforded me.

CONTENTS

Acknowledgements

Chapter 1 – Your Online Marketing Plan (Web Design, SEO, Online Reputation, Social Media, Email Marketing, PPC, Retargeting/Proximity Marketing, Content Creation)

Chapter 2 – Start with the fundamentals – Your Market, Message and Media

Chapter 3 – Web Design and Development – How to set up your website, platform options, navigation structure and user experience

Chapter 4 – Understanding How the Search Engines Work and the differences between the paid, organic and map listings

Chapter 5 – Search Engine Optimization – How to optimize your website for the keywords that are most important to your practice, How to conduct keyword research, our list of the most commonly searched keywords, how to optimize your website and pages for ranking, how to build authority on your website.

Chapter 6 – Google Maps Optimization – How to get ranked in Google map for your area, the fundamentals of ranking in the Google map pack, how to properly claim and optimize your GMB listing, how to develop authority with citations, how to get reviews from your patients

Chapter 7 – Website Conversion Fundamentals – How to ensure your visitors turn into patients for your practice

Chapter 8 – Mobile Optimization - How to optimize your website for mobile visitors

Chapter 9 – Online Reputation Management – How to ensure once someone finds you online, they know you are the practice they need to use

Chapter 10 – Social Media Marketing – How to leverage social media (FB, Twitter, Instagram and other platforms) for maximum effect in your practice

Chapter 11 – Video Marketing – How you can tap into the power of video online to enhance your visibility and drive better conversion

Chapter 12 – Email Marketing – How to leverage email and SMS marketing for more repeat and referral business

Chapter 13 – Pay Per Click – How Facebook, Instagram and other social media platform ads can drive a flood of new patients to your practice every month

Chapter 14 – Retargeting – How to increase the conversion rate of your website and ads around the web with retargeting

Chapter 15 – Proximity Marketing – How to target your potential patients based on where they frequent, pull patients from the big box stores to your practice

Chapter 16 – Content Marketing – How to position your practice as the leader in your market

Chapter 17 – Track, Measure and Quantify – How to track your online marketing plan and ensure your investment is generating a strong ROI

Next Steps

About the Author

Acknowledgements

I want to thank all the wonderful business and practice owners that have allowed me to hone my craft by working with their business. You know who you are and I could not have written this book without the real world experience that your company afforded me.

Chapter 1

Your Online Marketing Plan (Web Design, SEO, Online Reputation, Social Media, Email Marketing, PPC, Retargeting/Proximity Marketing, Content Creation, etc.)

Congratulations on your purchase of "The Complete Guide to Internet Marketing for Audiologists and Hearing Practices" a complete overview of what it takes to maximize your opportunities online.

There are a number of channels/mediums to consider for your practice when you look at the Online Marketing space. At first glance, considering all of the marketing options available in your online marketing playbook might be overwhelming. Search Engines (Organic, Maps, Pay-Per-Click), Social Media (Facebook, Twitter, Instagram, Youtube, etc.), Paid Online Directory Listings (Yelp, Yellowpages, BBB, etc.) and more. To maximize your patient flow from the Internet, you need to develop a PLAN that covers each of these online marketing opportunities. The purpose of this book is to outline a plan with that will transform you from an online marketing novice to the dominant player in your area. Throughout this book, we will lay the foundation to map out your online marketing plan:

- Your online marketing plan (Website, SEO, PPC, Email, Reputation etc.)
- How to setup your website to best serve your patients
- Understand how search engines work and learn the differences between the paid, organic and map listings
- Search Engine Optimization - How to optimize your website with keywords that are most important for your particular business
    - How to conduct Keyword Research
    - Our list of the most commonly searched keywords
    - How to achieve maximum result by mapping out the pages that should be included on your website
    - How to optimize your website for ranking in the organic listings on major Search Engines
    - How to improve your website's visibility so that you can rank on page one for your most important keywords
    - List of link building techniques and strategies that are proven to enhance rankings
    - Content marketing strategies for maintaining relevance in your market
- Google Maps Optimization - How to get ranked on the Google Map in your area
    - The fundamentals of Google Maps ranking (NAP, Citations, Consistency and Reviews)
    - How to establish a strong Name, Address, and Phone Number Profile
    - How to properly claim and optimize your Google My Business Local Listing
    - How to develop authority for your map listing via Citation Development

- List of the top citation sources for hearing practices
- How to get real reviews from your patients in your true service area
  - Sample Review Card
  - Sample Review Request Email
  - Sample Review Us landing page for your website
- Website Conversion Fundamentals - How to ensure that your website converts visitors into leads in the form of calls and web submissions
- Mobile Optimization - How to optimize your website for mobile visitors
- Social Media Marketing - How to utilize Social Media (Facebook, Twitter, Instagram, LinkedIn and other social platforms for maximum effect in your practice.
- Video Marketing - How to tap into the POWER of YouTube and other video sharing websites to enhance your visibility and drive better conversion
- Leverage email marketing tools (Constant Contact, Mail Chimp, etc) to connect with your patients on a deeper level, receive more reviews, get more social media connections and ultimately get repeat and referral business.
- Overview of Paid Online Advertising opportunities
- Pay-Per-Click Marketing (Google AdWords and Bing Search) - How to maximize the profitability of your Pay-Per-Click Marketing efforts
  - Why PPC should be part of your overall online marketing strategy
  - Why most PPC campaigns fail
  - Understanding the Google AdWords Auction process
  - How to configure and manage your Pay-Per-Click campaign for maximum ROI

- Paid Online Directories - What paid online directories should you consider advertising in (YP.com, Yelp.com, Merchant Circle, BBB.com, etc.)
- How to leverage retargeting and increase the conversion rate of your website and ads around the web
- Leverage Proximity marketing by targeting potential patients based on where they frequent
    - How to pull patients directly from the big box competitors into your practice
- Track, Measure and Quantify - How to track your online marketing plan to ensure that your investment is generating a strong ROI

When it comes to internet marketing for your practice, there are a number of avenues to explore. In this chapter, we will briefly touch on the various internet marketing channels that are available, and then go into more detail throughout the book. This chapter serves as your "Marketing Plan" and roadmap going forward.

Online Marketing Channels

1. Website
2. Search Engine Optimization (Organic Listings and Map Listings)
3. Online reputation management
4. Search Engine Marketing/PPC on Google AdWords and Bing Search Network
5. Social Media Marketing (Facebook, Twitter, Instagram, LinkedIn)
6. Video Marketing
7. Email Marketing
8. Retargeting/Proximity Marketing
9. Content Creation

Search Engine Optimization

Search Engine Optimization (SEO) is the process of increasing your company's visibility on major search engines (Google, Yahoo, Bing, etc.) in the organic, non-paid listings as consumers are searching for your products or services.

There are three very critical components of Search Engine Marketing. The three components are:

- Paid Listings – The area along the top and side that advertisers can bid on and pay for in order to obtain decent placement in the search engines.
- Organic Listings – The area in the body of the Search Engine Results page.
- Map Listings – These are the listings that come up beneath the paid listings and above the organic listings in a number of searches.

Search Engine Optimization involves getting your website to show up in the Organic and Map Listings. These listings account for a majority of the search volume. More than 91% of searchers click on the Organic (non-paid listings) rather than the paid listings. Read that again!

When most people think "Internet Marketing," they think Search Engine Optimization. However, you will begin to see that SEO is only a small piece of the MUCH BIGGER "Internet Marketing" puzzle for practices.

Search Engine Marketing / PPC

Now that we have discussed SEO, let's talk about Search Engine Marketing or PPC (Pay-Per-Click). Google, Yahoo and Bing all have paid programs that allow you to BUY listings associated with your keywords to be placed in designated areas of their sites. There are some stipulations to get your practice on Google and Bing PPC platforms but we will cover those later.

There are three really important benefits of PPC:

- Your keyword listings will appear on search engines almost immediately.
- You only have to pay when some actually clicks on your listing – hence the term Pay-Per-Click Marketing.
- You can get your ad to show up on national terms in the areas/cites in which you operate.

PPC Marketing works on an Auction system similar to that of eBay. You simply choose your keywords and propose a bid of what you would be willing to pay for each click. There are a number of factors that determine placement, which will be discussed in detail in the pay per click chapter. But, in the broadest sense, the practice who is willing to pay the most per click will be rewarded the top position in the search engines, while the second-most will be in the second position, etc.

PPC Marketing is a great way to get your company's website to appear at the top of the search engines right away, driving qualified traffic to your website.

Social Media Marketing

There is a lot of BUZZ around Social Media (Facebook, Twitter, Instagram, LinkedIn, YouTube), but how can it be utilized by a hearing practice? How can you use social media to grow your practice?

- More than 3.2 billion active social media users at the time of writing this
- 68% of U.S. adults report being active Facebook users
- The average person spends 2 hours and 22 minutes per day on social media
- 54% of social browsers use social media to research companies they want to do business with

So, how can you employ this amazing tool to grow your business? Use it to connect with your personal sphere of influence, past and new patients. By doing so, you can solidify and maintain existing relationships, remain Top-Of-Mind and ultimately Increase Repeat and Referral Business.

Video Marketing

Did you know that YouTube is the second-most used search engine on the market? Would you guess that it is ahead of Bing and Yahoo? It's true! Millions of people conduct YouTube searches on a daily basis. Most practices are so focused on SEO that they completely neglect the opportunities that video and YouTube provide. By implementing a Video Marketing Strategy for your business, you can get additional placement in search results for your keywords, enhance the effectiveness of your SEO efforts and improve visitor conversion.

Email Marketing

Similar to Social Media Marketing, Email Marketing is a great way to remain top-of-mind with your patients and increase repeat business and referrals. Compared to direct mail and newsletters, email marketing is by far the most cost effective means to communicate with your patients.

As we will discuss in the Email Marketing chapter, we feel that email marketing can be used to effectively draw your patients into your social media world.

Online Reputation

Half the battle online is being found, the other half is ensuring once a potential patient finds you – they know you are the practice they need to go to.

To accomplish this, your practice must have stellar reviews all around the web on platforms such as Google, Facebook, Yelp etc.

Proximity Marketing

You may have heard of this referred to as Geofencing but this is marketing to your potential patients based on where they are located or where they frequent.

This is an extremely powerful channel for practices because you can actually geofence and target competitors such as the big box brands. We will cover this in more detail in the proximity marketing chapter later.

Now that you have an understanding of each of the Internet Marketing Channels available, in the following chapters we will discuss how you can leverage them to connect with new patients and grow your practice.

WHERE TO START?

With such a large amount of internet marketing channels, where should you start? I firmly believe that over time, you should be appropriating each of these online marketing opportunities. However, you must first begin with the foundation - your website, organic rankings and social media/email. You should start looking at the various paid marketing opportunities when your website is setup correctly, ranking on search engines for your most important keywords in the organic, non-paid listings and you are actively engaging in social media activity. We have found that the biggest and most impactful opportunity is getting ranked organically (in the non-paid listings) along with social media marketing. You may then leverage the additional profits in paid marketing to further augment your growth. Once you are ranking well organically and things are firing on all cylinders, then you can start to run a well managed Pay-Per-Click Campaign and explore proximity marketing.

Next, lets look at the fundamentals of your overall marketing strategy before pressing forward into full implementation.

Chapter 2

Start With the Fundamentals – Your Market, Your Message, Your Media

Before we dive into Internet marketing, SEO and social media marketing and everything else I've outlined in this book, I want to be sure we have built a strong marketing foundation. As I talk with practice owners and managers across the United States, I have come to the realization that the vast majority of you tend to skip straight past the fundamentals of your marketing strategy and dive head-first into tactics (Web design, SEO, Social Media, etc.).

So, what do I mean when I say "Fundamentals"? All marketing has 3 core components:

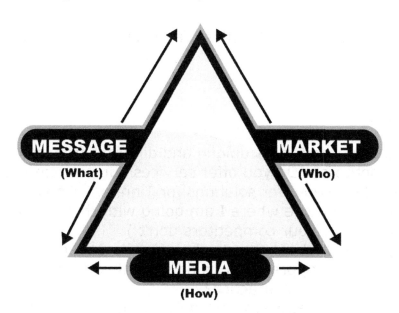

- Message (what)
- Market (who)
- Media (how)

You have to have a unique "Message" (who you are, what you do, what makes you unique, and why someone should use your practice over another), a specifically defined "Market" (who you sell to and who your BEST patients are), and THEN look at "Media" (where you can reach those BEST patients). The tactics (Pay-Per-Click, SEO, Social Media, Direct Mail, etc.) fall into the "Media" category.

If you focus solely on the Media or Tactics, you will likely fail regardless of how well selected that Media is. With that being said, you need to scale back to the fundamentals. You need to invest the time and energy in fleshing out your "Message" and figuring out who your "Market" is. By doing so, ALL of your Media choices will be vastly more effective. How can you do that?

Spend a few minutes and THINK. Take out a scratch pad and answer these questions:

Message:

- What do I do that is unique and different from my competitors? (Do you offer services your competitors don't? Do you offer solutions for Tinnitus? Do you deliver? You see where I am going with this. What do you do that your competitors don't.)
- If you think about the psychology of a patient, what concerns or apprehensions do you think they have about using your practice?
- How can you address your patients' common concerns in a unique way?

Market

- Who is my ideal patient? (Please realize that not everyone resides in your city nor within a 25 mile radius of your office is your ideal patient). You need to be clearer than that!
- Take a look at your last 25 patients and evaluate who spent the most money, who had the highest profit margins and who was genuinely pleased with your service. What are the unique characteristics of those good patients? Are they homeowners vs. renters? Do they live in a particular area of town? Do they have a higher income level?
- Start to define who your ideal patient is so that you can put a marketing plan in place to attract similar patients.

Once you have ironed out your Message and your Market you can start to think about Media. In order to determine what media will be most effective for you, you need to think about where you can reach your IDEAL patient.

Clearly, the Internet is a great "media" for connecting with your ideal patient who is proactively in the market for your services. Throughout the remainder of this book, we will be explaining the various Internet marketing channels and how you can use them to connect with your ideal patient.

Remember, you need to start with the FUNDAMENTALS (Message, Market and Media) before running headstrong into any marketing endeavor.

Chapter 3

Web Design and Development – How to set up your website, platform options, navigation structure and user experience

This chapter is all about how to setup your website. We are going to cover a lot of details as they relate to SEO, Google Maps Optimization, Social Media Marketing, etc. However, without a properly designed and functioning website, those efforts will be put to waste. Before you can or even should begin exploring those options, you must have your website up and running.

Let's talk about website formats and the different options that are available to you when you are ready to start.
1. HTML Site – There are basic HTML pages and/or individual pages that can be incorporated into a website. This is how almost all websites were built several years ago. They had multiple pages hyper-linked together.
2. Template Based Site Builders - Site builders, that you can obtain through providers such as Go Daddy, Squarespace, Wix and Weebly are turnkey. You buy your domain and set up your website. I have found this type to be quite a bit less than ideal because you don't have a lot of control or flexibility. But, there are still a lot of sites in this format.
3. CMS Systems - Content Management Systems, like WordPress, Joomla, Drupal. I'm sure there are many others but these are the big ones.

As far as I'm concerned, a content management system is ideal for your practice website. The reason that I say that is because you have scalability. In any of these platforms, you have the ability to change your navigation on the fly, add as many pages as you need and easily scale out your site. If you have your website built in HTML format with graphics behind the website, and you wanted to add a new section, you would have to start from scratch. You would have to go back to the graphics and modify all of the pages in order to add the new section to your navigational structure. With a CMS, everything is built behind code allowing the ability to apply easy edits and to add multiple pages.

As you will see in the search engine optimization section of the book, you will have the ability to have a page for each one of your services and each city that you operate in. A CMS allows you to create your pages in a scalable format without having to mess around with the graphics or do anything that is difficult to control. Also, it is easy to access, modify, and update. Using formats like WordPress and Joomla, you may access the back-end administrative area at *yourpractice.com/login.* After entering your username and password, you will find that there is a very easy to edit system with pages and posts that function similarly to Microsoft Word. You can input text, import images and press "save," forcing all new edits to be updated on your live website. It is easier than it looks and is very search engine friendly.

Content Management Systems have intelligently structured linking between pages and content, making it extremely search engine friendly. We have found that this method tends to be better than regular HTML or template based builder options. In a lot of cases, a blog is going to be automatically bolted onto a CMS based website providing you with a section where you may feed updates. In the SEO chapter, we cover the importance of creating consistent updates and blogging regularly.

Another benefit of content management systems is that you are provided with a variety of plugins that you can choose to incorporate on your website. You can easily pull in your social media feeds, YouTube Videos and check-ins. You may also syndicate your website to automatically post any new updates to your social media profiles. You can add map integration where people can click to get directions directly to your location. There are a surplus of features available within a CMS that you can't necessarily do with a non-CMS type option.

Whether you are looking to build a website from the ground up, if you are just getting started, or you feel like you simply need a redesign, I highly suggest that you do so in a content management system: ideally in WordPress. WordPress is a fantastic platform and very easy to use. It's the most adopted website platform available with a lot of developers working on it. It's constantly being updated and improved and I have found it to work very well for practices.

What should your website have?

So, what should your website have? What navigation structure should you create? You definitely want to have:
1. Home

2. About Us
3. Our Services
4. Patient Portal Integration
5. FAQ
6. Book Appointment
7. Online Specials or Coupons
8. Reviews and Testimonials
9. Blog
10. Contact Us

These are the core pages. Within "About Us," you might incorporate a drop down menu for subcategories including "Meet the Team," "Why Choose Our Practice," etc. I think that's very powerful.

You want to be able to drive people back to a "Why Choose Us" section, and, in some cases, if you are having issues recruiting and retaining good quality talent, you might want to have a "Careers" page under the "About Us" navigation, where a visitor can go and fill out an application and learn more about your organization. Within "Our Services," you want to have the ability to list a drop down listing the types of services that you offer. We discuss this to a great extent in the SEO module. You want to have landing pages for each one of your services because they are going to be optimized with different keyword combinations.

A "Reviews and Testimonials" page will provide you with a section to showcase what your patients are saying about you in text or video form. You can also pull in reviews from sites such as Google, Facebook, and Yelp. Finally, of course, you will need a "Contact Us" page where web visitors have your general contact information.

These are the core things you should have on your website.

Outside of your navigational structure, what else should your website have? What other elements are going to help with conversion? Well, you should always provide a primary phone number on every page of your website, in the right hand corner. So, when somebody visits a page, their eyes are naturally drawn to the top section of the website, the logo and the phone number. People tend to expect that phone number will be somewhere in this location. It is ideal to have a prominent phone number, telling them to call you now.

I believe that practice websites should always make a web form available from which a patient can easily book an appointment. Bear in mind that every visitor to your website is in a different situation and frame of mind. You may have someone that's on their phone or just leisurely looking to contact you for various hearing services and is able to simply pick up the phone and call you. On the other hand, somebody that's in a work environment may not have the ability to stop what they are doing and make a phone call without drawing attention from his or her coworkers. However, they may be able to browse around online to find out what options are available. Your potential patients reach your website and they are torn between making a call right at that moment, submitting a form, or wanting to have someone from your team contact them. Make it easy for them to enter their information into a web form where they can provide their name, phone number, email address, and prescription information that they can send through online. It makes it easier and doesn't create any pressure.

You also want to provide links to your social media profiles. Link to Facebook, Twitter, Instagram and LinkedIn so patients can easily jump off, engage with you on social media, see what you're doing and be able to press that important "like," "follow" or "subscribe" button. It helps create a sense of authenticity when your patients get to see your social media content.

Have a direct link that drives visitors to your online reviews and testimonials that we discussed previously. You should also post your credentials either in the sidebar or in the header graphic, proving, for example, that you're BBB-accredited or a member of the local chamber of commerce or industry association. This allows potential patients to rest assured that you are a credible organization, that you're involved in the community and that you're less apt to provide them with ill-service. They'll feel more comfortable doing business with you.

You definitely need to have your company name, address and phone number on every page of your website. It is not critical that you list your address on each page because it will not be a determining factor in whether or not they call you, but as I will explain in the Google Maps optimization chapter, having name, address and phone number consistency is critical for ranking on the Google Map.
It is a great strategy to have your name, address and phone number referenced on your website, ideally in the footer section. You need to have that contact information on all of your pages including the Contact Us page, of course.

It's extremely important that you infuse personality into your website. By personality, I'm referring to authentic photos and videos. Showcase your company, feature yourself, the business owner, and the people that work in the business; the specialists, the office team, etc. Showcase the practice itself, because patients will be coming there. Don't use stock photography, but authentic imagery. This gives the visitor the chance to get to know, like and trust you, before they even pick up the phone. I've seen this tactic prove itself time and time again.

Say a potential patient visited two different sites. One of them is generic; here's the same image he or she has seen before of the same hearing instrument specialist fitting a guy with a hearing aid with the same smile. The other website highlights a genuine picture of the owner, the team and the practice. This authentic page converts 10 to 1. You must let your real personality reflect on the website.

You must also craft messaging that explains why they should choose your practice. Why should someone choose you over the competition? Pull them down a path where they can start to learn more about why you are they're best option. Where they can see your online reviews, and if they're kind of on the fence, where they can quickly locate some special offers and incentives that will drive action. That will get them to contact you right away, as opposed to continuing to browse the web for someone else.

The other major thing you want to think about, from the conversion perspective, is having a mobile-ready version of your website. More and more people are accessing the Internet via smart phones such as iPhones and Android phones. Mobile website traffic has actually surpassed desktop traffic. You need to make sure that the mobile version of your site isn't the same as your regular site. It should be condensed, fitting their screen and giving them just the information that they need. It should integrate with their phone so all they have to do is press a button to call you. People that are searching or accessing your website from a mobile device are in a different state of mind than the people that are browsing and finding you on a computer. Make it easy for them to get the information they need and to get in touch with you.

Chapter 4

Understanding How the Search Engines Work and the differences between the paid, organic and map listings

In this section, we wanted to take a few minutes to demystify the search engines and break down the anatomy of the Search Engine Results Page. By understanding how each component works, you can formulate a strategy to maximize your results.

There are three core components of the Search Engines Results page:

1. Paid/PPC Listings
2. Map Listings
3. Organic Listings

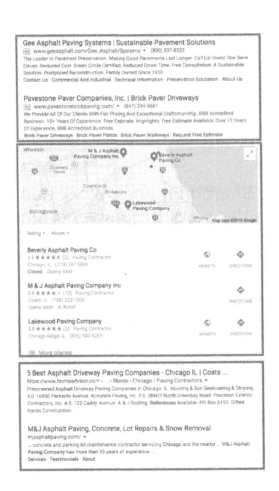

1. Paid Results
2. Local Results
3. Organic Results

1. Paid/PPC Listings – In the paid section of the search engines you are able to select keywords that are relevant to your business, and then pay to be listed amongst the search results. The reason it is referred to as PPC or Pay-Per-Click is because rather than paying a flat monthly or daily fee for placement, you simply pay each time someone clicks on the link.
2. Map Listings – The map listings have become very important because they are the first thing that comes up in search results for most locally based searches. If

someone searches "hearing aids + your city," chances are the map listings will be the first thing they look at. Unlike the paid section of the search engine, you can't buy your way into the Map Listings. You have to earn it. Once you do, there is no per-click cost associated with being in this section of the search engine.
3. Organic Listings – The organic/natural section of the Search Engine Results page appears directly beneath the Map Listings in many local searches, but appears directly beneath the Paid Listings in the absence of the Map Listings (the Map Section only shows up in specific local searches). Similar to the Map Listings, you can't pay your way into this section of the search engines and there is no per-click cost associated with it.

Now that you understand the three major components of the Search Engine Results and the differences between Paid Listings, Map Listings and Organic Listings you might wonder... "What section is the most important?" This is a question that we receive from practices every day.

The fact is that all three components are important, and each should have a place in your online marketing program because you want to show up as often as possible when someone is searching for hearing aids in your area. With that said, assuming you are operating on a limited budget and need to make each marketing dollar count, you need to focus your investment on the sections that are going to drive the strongest Return On Investment.

Research indicates that the vast majority of the population looks directly at the Organic and Map Listings when conducting a search, and their eyes simply glance over the Paid Listings.

So, if you are operating on a limited budget and need to get the best bang for your buck, you should start by focusing your efforts on the area that gets the most clicks at the lowest cost. We have found that placement in the Organic and Map section on the Search Engines drive a SIGNIFIGANTLY higher Return On Investment than Pay-Per-Click Marketing.

Begin with the Organic Listings and then, as you increase your profits, you can start to shift those dollars into a proactive Pay-Per-Click Marketing effort.

In the next chapter, we will start to look at Search Engine Optimization and how to optimize your website to rank in the organic listings (non-paid) for the most important keywords in your business.

Chapter 5

Search Engine Optimization – How to optimize your website for the keywords that are most important to your practice, How to conduct keyword research, our list of the most commonly searched keywords for hearing practices, how to optimize your website and pages for ranking, how to build authority on your website.

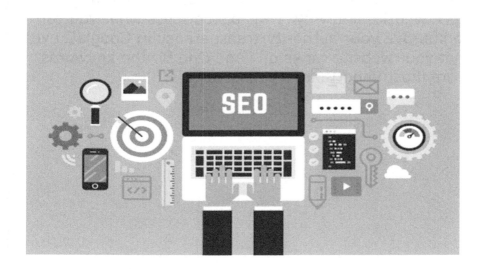

Getting your practice listed in the organic section (non-paid-listings) of the Search Engines comes down to two core factors:

- Having the proper on-page optimization so that Google knows what you do and the general area that you serve. This allows it to put in the index for the right keywords. You do this by having pages for each of your services and then optimizing them for specific keyword combinations (Ex. Your City + main service, Your City + service 2, Your City + service 3, etc.).
- Creating enough authority and transparency so that Google ranks you on Page One (rather than page ten) for those specific keywords. Ultimately, it comes down to having credible inbound links and citations from other websites to your website and it's sub-pages. He who has the most credible inbound links, citations and reviews will be the most successful.

Throughout the course of this chapter I will provide specific how-to information on exactly what pages to add to your practice website and why. I will also discuss what you can do to improve your authority/transparency in Google's eyes so that your website ranks on Page One for the keywords that are most important to your business.

Before you start creating pages and trying to do the "on-page optimization" work, you need to be clear on the most commonly searched keywords relative to the services you offer. By understanding the keywords, you can be sure to optimize your website for the words that will actually drive qualified traffic to your site. Our team has done a great deal of due diligence and developed the following list of the most commonly searched keywords for hearing practices and audiologists, listed at the end of this chapter.

If you happen to work in a different industry than what is listed and you wish to learn the methodology behind selecting these keywords, we have provided an overview of how to conduct keyword research.

How to conduct Keyword Research to determine what your patients are searching when they need your services.

There are a number of tools that can be used to conduct keyword research. Some are free of charge and others have a monthly cost associated with them. Some of the better keyword research tools include Wordstream, Google

AdWords Keyword Tool, Keywords Everywhere and Keywordtool.io.

For the purposes of this book, we have developed instructions based on the site Keywordtool.io.

- Develop a list of your services and save it in a .txt file
- Develop a list of the cities that you operate in (your primary city of service and the smaller surrounding towns) and save it in a .txt file
- Go to www.mergewords.com
    - Paste your list of cities in column 1
    - Paste your list of services in column 2
    - Press the "Merge!" button
    - The tool will generate a list of all your services combined with your cities of service
- Go to keywordtool.io
    - Paste your list of merged keywords into the "word or phrase" box
    - Press "Submit"
- You will now see a list of each of your keywords with a "search volume" number beside it
- Sort the list from greatest to smallest

You now have a list of the most commonly searched keywords in your area.

With this list you can map out keywords to specific pages on your website and rest assured that you are basing your strategy on opportunity rather than a guestimate.

Below you will find the list of the most commonly searched keywords for hearing practices and audiologists.

Most Search Audiology and Hearing Keywords:

Hearing Aids	140,000
Hearing Aids Near Me	1,800
Audiologist	74,000
Audiologist Near Me	3,300
Hearing doctor	2,100
Hearing doctor near me	1,500
Hearing aids cost	9,900
Hearing aid price	3,100

Based on this data, in order to get the most from the internet from a SEO perspective, you will want to create content on your website for the following keyword combinations:

- Your City + hearing aids near me
- Your City + hearing aids
- Your City + audiologist
- Your City + audiologist near me
- Your City + hearing doctor
- Your City + hearing care

How to map out the pages on your website for maximum result

Now that you are set to determine the most commonly searched keywords in your field, you can begin mapping out the pages that need to be added to your website.

Keep in mind that each page on your website can only be optimized for 1-2 keyword combinations. If you came up with 25 keywords then you are going to need at least 12 – 15 landing pages.

You need to be sure you have each keyword mapped to a specific page on your site.

Keyword	Mapped to what page
Main Keyword	Home
Keyword 1	Services - Keyword 1
Keyword 2	Services - Keyword 2
Keyword 3	Services - Keyword 3
Keyword 4	Services - Keyword 4
Keyword 5	Services - Keyword 5

Now that you have mapped out the pages that need to be included on your website, you can start thinking about how to optimize each of those pages for the major search engines (Google, Yahoo and Bing).

How to optimize your website and pages for ranking in the organic listings on Search Engines

Step 1 – Build the website and obtain more placeholders on the major search engines.

A typical practice website has only 5-6 pages (Home – About Us – Our Services – FAQ – Contact Us). That does not create a lot of indexation or placeholders on the major search engines. Most practices provide a wide variety of services, so creating pages for those services is the best route. By building out the website and creating separate pages that highlight each of these services that are offered (combined with city modifiers), the practice can get listed on the search engines for each of those different keyword combinations.

Step 2 – Optimize Pages for Search Engines:

Once the pages and sub-pages are built for each of your core services, each page needs to be optimized from an SEO perspective in order to make the search engines understand what the page is about. Here are some of the most important items that need to be taken care of for on-page search engine optimization:

- Unique Title Tag on each page
- H1 Tag restating that Title Tag on each page
- Images named with primary keywords
- URL containing page keyword
- Anchor Text on each page and built into Footer
- XML Sitemap should be created and submitted to Google Webmaster Tools and Bing Webmaster Tools

How to build up the authority of your website so you can rank on page one for your most important keywords

Once the pages are built and the "on-page" SEO is complete, the next step is getting inbound links. Everything we have discussed to this point is sort of like laying the groundwork –the pages need to be in order to even be in the running. However, it is the number of QUALITY inbound links and web references to those pages that is going to determine placement.

30% of SEO is On-Page type work
The other 70% is Link Building

Once the pages are built is just the beginning. The only way to get your site to rank above your competition is by having MORE quality inbound links and citations to your site.

He Who Has The MOST Quality Inbound Links WINS!

Again, if there is any secret sauce to ranking well in the search engines, it really is links, trust and authority. The major caveat to that is that you can't just use garbage links. You don't want to just have a thousand links. When I say links, I'm referring to other websites hyper-linking to your website, which I'll explain a little bit more with specific examples.

The latest algorithm changes involve Google trying to prevent spam. A lot of internet marketers and SEO coordinators realize it's all about the links. That is what the Google algorithm was built upon. They figured out ways to get a variety of links with random anchor text pointed back to the pages that they want to have ranked. Google has recognized that if those links are not relevant then they don't add any value to the internet.

Bad or irrelevant links can actually hurt your ranking more than help it. It's about getting quality, relevant links back to your home page and sub-pages through content creation and strategic link-building. How do you get the links? Where do you get the links?

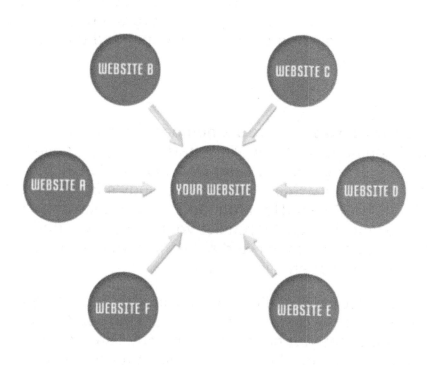

1. Association Links – Be sure that you have a link to your site from any industry associations that you belong to (Ex. AAA, ADA, Your State Assoc. etc.).

2. Directory Listings – Get your site listed on as many directory type websites as possible (Yelp, Merchant Circle, Yellowpages etc.)
3. Create Interesting Content/Articles about your industry. This is probably the #1 source of inbound links. For example, you can write an article about "tinnitus" and push it out to thousands of people through article directory sites that may each contain a link back to a specific page on your site.
4. Competitive Link Acquisition – this is the process of using tools like Raven Tools, SEO Book and others to see what links your top competitors have, and then get those same or similar links pointed back to your website.

Directory Links - There's a number of what I like to call "low-hanging fruit" links. It all starts with your online directory listings. Some examples include Google Maps, Yahoo Local, City Search, Yelp.com, Judy's Book, Best of the Web, Yellow Pages, Hot Frog, and the list goes on. All of those online listings let you list your company name, address, phone number and a link back to your website. Some of them even allow reviews.

For the most part, adding your business information to those directories is completely free of charge. You want to make sure that you have your company listed on as many of the online directory listings as possible for authoritative linking reasons.

They're also valuable from the Google Maps optimization perspective because they give you citations, which are very important for getting ranked on the map. A great way to find additional online directories to add your company to would be to run a search in Google for "Your Company Type

– Business Directory" or "Your City – Business Directory". This will give you a great list of potential directory sites to add your company to. There are also tools for this like BrightLocal or White Spark, that can provide you with a list of directory sources based on your industry. After beginning with online directory listings, you want to look at any associations that you're involved with.

Association Links –I'm assuming you are involved in some type of association, whether it is the national industry association, the local chapter or some other group affiliation. Visit the websites of those organizations and get listed in the member section. This will give you citations and the opportunity to link back to your website.

Affiliated Industries and Local Businesses that are non-competitive - You can work with colleagues that have affiliated industry type businesses. Utilizing your resources and teaming up with relevant companies will add more authority to your domain.

Social Media Profile Links - The other "low-hanging fruit" links are social media profiles. We have a whole chapter about the power of social media and how you can harness it to get repeat and referral business. Simply from a link-building perspective, you should set up a Facebook page, Twitter account, LinkedIn profile, Instagram page, Pinterest profile and a You Tube channel and place a link to your website on each. Each one of them will allow you to enter your company's name, address, phone number a description and, of course, a place to put your website address.

Local Association - Other local associations that you're involved in. If you're a member of the Chamber of Commerce, a networking group like BNI (Business Networking International), or if you're involved with a local charity, find out if they list their members on their websites.

Another great place to get links is by typing in your city directory.

Competitive Link Acquisition - You might be surprised that if you really tackle these elements and you don't do any of the other things we have discussed, you will notice that you've probably got enough links to outrank your competition in your area. I want to share some additional thoughts and strategies on how you can accomplish even more from a link building perspective. A very powerful strategy that you can implement is called Competitive Link Acquisition.

The way I like to think of it is that if quantity inbound links are the secret sauce to outranking your competition, and if we could figure out who's linking to your competition or what links your competition have, and we can get those same or similar links pointed back to your website, then you can outrank them, because you'll at that point have more authority. Competitive link acquisition is the process of figuring out who is in the top position for your most important keywords, reverse engineering their link profile to see what links they have, and getting those same or similar links pointed back to your website. A simple way to do this is just to go to Google.com and type in "your city + audiologist," and find out who is in the top few positions. Let's take a look at the number one placeholder. He's there because his website is optimized well and Google knows that he should be ranked well based on the quality and quantity inbound links compared to the competition.

Once you know who he is, you can use a couple of different tools such as Raven Tools, Majestic SEO, SEM Rush etc., and you can take their URL, input it into your tool of choice, run the report, and get a list of links in return.

So, your number one competitor is xyzpractice.com. Google spits out a list showing that they have 392 inbound links.

- He's got a link from the local Chamber of Commerce.
- He's got a link from the ADA.
- He's got a link from an article that he posted in the local newspaper.
- He's got a link from the local networking chapter.

By analyzing the types of links that he has, you can systematically mimic those links and get them pointed back to your website.

Don't just do this for your first competitor, but also for your second and third and fourth and fifth competitors. By doing that on a consistent basis, you can start to dominate the search engines for your most important keywords.

If you build out your site for your services and sub-services, optimize the pages using SEO best practices and then systematically obtain inbound links, you will start to DOMINATE the search engines for the hearing related keywords in your area.

Content marketing strategies for maintaining relevance in your market

Another highly important factor in SEO is relevant ongoing updates to your website. In the Internet age, content is king.

Google loves fresh content. In some cases, with the changes in the algorithm, just because you've got a great website with the right title tags and all the best links, you may get discounted if they're not seeing fresh information posted on a consistent basis. It is important to have a methodology where you are creating and posting content to your website on a regular basis. I want to give you a framework for figuring out what kind of content you could write, why you should create content, and how you can do it consistently.

First, you need to understand and accept that you need to become a subject matter expert. You might not consider yourself a writer or a content creator, but you are a subject matter expert.

There are things that you know that the general population does not. You're a hearing expert and you have a team of people that are experts in this area as well. You can create content on the topic that you know most about.

You can write about the differences between hearing aids, the importance of hearing tests, or any other common questions you may get often. There are a lot of different topics you can come up with that you can create content about.

You should also consider that content doesn't have to be just written words. It's doesn't have to be just articles. Content can come in a variety of forms. The most popular are going to be articles, photos, videos and audio files. Stop and think about what content creation method works best for you.

Some people are great writers and that's their strength. Other people like to be on camera. I personally like to create videos. I'm very comfortable creating videos.

Other people can talk, and they can talk your ear off about whatever topic they are passionate about. You can create content in many different ways. Because it is what I enjoy, I'll use video as an example. A practice can set up a camera and record themselves explaining the benefits of hearing tests and why they are necessary.

Now you'll actually have multiple pieces of content. You'll have a video, which can be uploaded to You Tube, Vimeo, etc. That one piece of content can create multiple invaluable links to your website.

You can also take that video, save the audio portion of it, and you've got an audio clip. You can upload that audio file to your website and post on other various sites. You can use a transcription service like Castingwords.com, for instance, where you upload the audio or video file and somebody converts it to text. For a couple of bucks, you'll have a complete article comprised of what you said. Now you've got a piece of content you can post to your blog.

You want to create content on a consistent basis, using the blog on your website as the hub to post it, but then syndicating it to various sources. Syndicating it to article directory sites if it's in text form, and sending it to video sites like Vimeo and YouTube.com if it's in video form. Doing this keeps the content fresh on your website/domain and creates a lot of authority, which is really going to help with the overall ranking of the website on the search engines.

You want to make sure you're appropriating each one of these link-building opportunities to maximize your rank-potential in your area. There are a lot of practices that want to rank for the same keywords, and many of them have invested heavily in the internet and in getting themselves higher in the search engines.

Now that you've built out your website, you've optimized it correctly, and you've got an ongoing link-building and content development strategy in place, you want to start looking at Google Maps Optimization and getting ranked on the Google Map.

Chapter 6

Google Maps Optimization – How to get ranked in the Google map for your area, the fundamentals of ranking in the Google map pack, how to properly claim and optimize your GMB listing, how to develop authority with citations, how to get reviews from your patients

The fundamentals of Google Maps ranking (NAP, Citations, Consistency and Reviews)

Getting listed on the first page of the Google Map for "Your City + Service" comes down to four primary factors:

- Having a claimed and verified Google My Business
- Having an optimized Google My Business profile listing for the area that you operate in
- Having a consistent N.A.P. (Name, Address, Phone Number Profile) across the web so that Google feels confident that you are a legitimate organization located in the place you have listed and serving the market you claim to serve.
- Having reviews from your patients in your service area

If you have each of these four factors working in your favor you will SIGNIFICANTLY improve the probability of ranking on page one of Google Maps in your market.

How to establish a strong Name, Address, Phone Number Profile

As I mentioned above, having a consistent Name, Address, Phone Number Profile across the web is essential for ranking well on the Google Map in your area. Google sees it as a signal of authority.

Rather than jumping directly into claiming your Google Map listing and citation-building, it's critical that you start by determining your true N.A.P. so that you can ensure that it is referenced consistently across the web.

When I say making sure that it's consistent, you want to be certain that you are always referencing the legitimate name for your business. If your company's name is "XYZ Practice", you must always list it as "XYZ Practice," and not abbreviate or alter it.

The other thing you should be aware of is that there is a lot of misinformation about how to list your company name online. You may read information suggesting that you keyword your name. For example, if your name is "XYZ Practice," somebody might tell you it would be really smart if you just added to the title of your company "XYZ Practice | Dallas Audiologist," for instance. While that may have worked back in the day, it's no longer an effective strategy. It's actually a violation of Google policies and procedures. Make sure you list your exact company name the same way across the board on all of your directory sources. Also make sure that you use the same phone number in all of those places. I'm a big advocate for tracking phone numbers and what is happening with your marketing. But, when it comes to your online directory listings, you want to use your primary business phone number that you've been using from the beginning.

Don't try to create some unique number for each one of your directories. What that does is confuses your name/address profile. It will hurt you. Use your primary phone number in all of those places, use your exact company name, and use your principal address, written the same way. If your business is located at "1367 South West 87th Street, Suite Number 105," make sure you list it just like that every single time. Don't neglect to include the suite in one place and then put it on in another. Don't spell out "South West" in one place and put "SW" in the other. We are driving for a consistent name/address profile across the web.

A good way to figure out what Google considers to be your N.A.P. is to run a search on Google for "Your Practice" and see what is being referenced on the Google Map. See how that compares to the other high authority sites like YP.com, Yelp.com, Merchant Circle and others. Look for the predominant combination of N.A.P. and reference that for all your directory work going forward.

How to properly claim and optimize your Google My Business Listing

Below you will find a step-by-step guide for checking, claiming and managing your Local Business Listings on Google.

1. Setup a new Google account or sign into yours, if you already have one.

2. Head to https://www.google.com/business and click Start Now

3. Enter Your Business Name. If you see your business appear on the drop down menu, click it and proceed by claiming the existing listing. If you do not see your business appear on the drop down, Google does not have an existing listing for your practice.

4. Enter your business address. If you offer delivery services, click the box labeled 'I deliver goods and services to my patients location'. DO NOT CHECK THE BOX TO HIDE YOUR ADDRESS. Finally, select the delivery area.

5. Choose Your Business Category - this will be audiologist or hearing aid store. You will be able to choose other categories later on but this will be your main one.

6. Add Your Business Phone Number and Website

7. Choose Your Verification option and verify your listing!

- Postcard
- Phone
- Email
- Instant Verification

Instant Verification is not available for all business categories. You will most likely have to use one of the first 3 options. I recommend phone or email, since they are much faster than postcard.

How to Optimize Your Google My Business Listing

Enter Complete Data for Your Listing

Local search results favor the most relevant results for searches, and business offering the most detailed and accurate information will be easier to serve in search.

Don't leave anything to be guessed or assumed; make sure your listing communicates with potential patients what your business does, where it is, and how they can acquire the good and/or services your business is offering.

Include Keywords

Just like traditional website SEO, Google uses a variety of signals to serve search results, and including important keywords and search phrases to your business listing will be incredibly helpful, especially since your business website is listed directly within your GMB listing.

Keep Business Operating Hours Accurate

It's important to enter your business hours, but equally important to update them whenever they change.

Google offers the ability to customize hours for holidays and other special events, and it should always be used to keep your site accurate and users happy.

Add Photos

Photos help business listings' performance more than most business owners and marketers probably expect.

Businesses with photos on their listings receive 42 percent more requests for driving directions on Google Maps and 35 percent more click-throughs to their websites than businesses that without photos, according to Google.

Manage & Respond to Patient Reviews

Interacting with patients by responding to their reviews illustrates that your business values its patients and the feedback that they leave regarding it.

Positive reviews are going to have a positive effect on potential patients when researching your business, but they also increase your business's visibility in search results.

Encourage patients to leave feedback by creating a link they can click to write reviews for your business.

How to develop authority for your map listing via Citation Development

Now that you have claimed your Google My Business Listing and optimized it to its fullest, you need to build authority. Having a well-claimed and optimized Google My Business listing doesn't automatically rank you on page one. Google wants to list the most legitimate and qualified providers first. So, how do they figure out who gets the page one listings? Well, there are a number of determining factors, but one of them is how widely the company is referenced on various online directory sites such as Yellow Pages, City Search, Yelp and others.

Citations are web references to your company name, address and phone number. You can add citations in a variety of ways. There are directory listings that you should claim manually and others that you can submit to via submission services like Bright Local or Yext.com. My personal preference is to claim listings manually, ensuring that I am in control and can make updates/edits as needed.

TOP Citation Sources to claim manually:

- Google My Business
- Bing Local
- Yahoo Local
- City Search
- Angie's List
- Yelp
- YP.com
- Merchant Circle
- Manta

List of the top citation sources for practices

1		Google My Business
2		Bing Places
3		Apple Maps
4		Infogroup
5		LocalEze
6		Factual
7		Foursquare
8		Facebook
9		D&B
10		Yelp
11		Yellowpages
12		CityGrid
13		MapQuest
14		Superpages
15		Manta
16		Local.com
17		Yellowbook

18	ChamberofCommerce
19	Merchantcircle
20	BOTW
21	Opendi
22	HotFrog
23	Brownbook
24	Cylex
25	InsiderPages
26	EZLocal
27	Tupalo
28	CitySquares
29	GetFave
30	2FindLocal
31	Fyple
32	Here
33	Angieslist
34	BBB

35	BizVotes
36	Yahoo! Local
37	DexKnows
38	n49
39	Thumbtack
40	Infobel
41	eLocal
42	Tuugo
43	BizJournals
44	B2BYellowpages
45	ThreeBestRated
46	MyHuckleberry
47	SaleSpider
48	ShowMeLocal
49	Yasabe
50	Cybo

By securing these high quality citations you will boost your authority and highly improve your probability of ranking in the Google Map Listings. The next critical step is to get online reviews!

How to get online reviews. Real reviews from your real patients.

The next critical component for getting ranked on the Google Map, after you've claimed and optimized your listing, you've established your N.A.P. and you've developed your citations across the web, is obtaining reviews. You need to have real reviews from your real patients.

First, I want to point out that you shouldn't fill the system with fake or fraudulent reviews. You do not want to create bogus accounts and post reviews to Google Map, Yelp, City Search, etc. just for the sake of saying you've got reviews. That's not going to help you. You need real reviews from your actual patients.

You might be thinking "Well, how is that important?" or "How would Google know the difference?" Google is paying very close attention to the reviewer's profile.

If somebody is an active Google user and they've got a Gmail account, and they've got a YouTube channel, typically that's all connected to a Google profile.

Say that person with the active profile has had their account for seven years and actually happens to be located in your service area. If he or she writes you a review, it would be considered credible and will count in your favor. Now, if somebody creates a Google account with the sole intent of writing a review, it obviously is not credible and Google is capable of catching on to that. That account has no history associated with it and it was originated right at your office IP address. That review is going to be flagged as a bogus submission.

It is important to have an authentic strategy where you are connecting with real people who will write your reviews. You don't want to try and play the system. Google is fully aware, and so is Yelp and a number of other popular online review sites.

With that said, how can you get reviews? What kind of process will you need to actually get reviews from your real patients? Here's the strategy that we advocate.

For our clients, we rely on software to facilitate this entire process. First, we develop a "Feedback page" which the practice will have on pulled up on a tablet that sits at the front desk. The patient enters their Name, Email and Phone Number and hits 'Submit". This landing page looks like this:

The software allows for the practice to collect feedback from actual patients. Once they go through the pages on the tablet in the practice, they receive an email about an hour later asking the patient to send the review to Google.

The great thing about this software is we have the capability of filtering the reviews. This means if a patient were to leave a low feedback score, we would them send them to a feedback page where we can learn more about why they gave us the poor review.

This allows the practice to gauge how well their team is doing with the patients and use this for quality control measures. This software is a not solely focused on just Google reviews either. The idea is to use this for all review platforms such as Bing, Yelp, etc.

If you follow these steps to properly claim your Google Map listing, develop your authority via citation development and put a systematic process in place to get real reviews from your real patients, you will be well on your way to dominating the Google Map listings in your market.

Chapter 7

Website Conversion Fundamentals – How to ensure your visitors turn into repeat patients for your practice

This chapter is all about website conversion fundamentals; about how you need to set up your website, the messaging on your website, the navigational flow of your website, to ensure maximum conversion and profitability from your entire online marketing effort.

The way I look at it is, you can have the best Pay-Per-Click campaign, search engine optimization, and be ranked number one on the Google Map. But, if the content and the structure of your website isn't set up in a way that's compelling for users, then it doesn't give them a reason to choose you over the competition, and it doesn't give them the information that they need to easily say, "You're the company that I am going to call for help." It's just not going to do as well as it could. I want to talk about how we can take the traffic we're going to get from organic and Pay-Per-Click strategies, and make sure that the website is illustrating the correct message so we can maximize the profitability and revenue of our online marketing strategies.

Be real. I talked about how people resonate with real people. They like to see the company, the people that they are going to be talking with on the phone and who they will see in the practice. So, as often as you can, avoid stock photography. Get a picture of the owner, the team, and practice itself.

These things really draw people in and it gets them to feel see that they would be working with real people because that is the kind of business that people want to deal with. As for the content of your website, write messaging that draws them in and makes them connect. They're looking for a practice that they know will take care of them, so when they land on your homepage, the first message they see should enforce the fact that they can trust you. You should write something along the lines of, "Are you looking for a company that you can trust? Then you've come to the right place. We're operating on the same principles for the last 30 years: trust, innovation, and excellence."

Connect with them. Give them reasons to choose you and have a call-to-action, "Give us a call at this number for immediate service," or, "Click here to take advantage of our online specials and discounts." Remember, they've browsed around the internet and have seen that there are dozens of companies that they can choose from.

Give them some compelling information about who you are and why they would want to choose you. Ask them to book an appointment now or to speak with the audiologist. This is going to propel them to choose you and make that call right away.

When it comes to the copy on the website, you want to address their specific concerns. On the home page, write something generic, "Looking for a practice you can trust?" On specific service pages, speak to their frustrations. For example on the services page, speak to the frustration of having to change the batteries on their hearing aids.

Write that kind of messaging for each one of the pages on your website including a clear call to action after every block of text. Pull them deeper into your website with "About Us" links, special offers, etc.

Give them content that makes them think, "These guys know what they're doing," and draw them deeper and deeper into the website so they're more inclined to take the next step. Tell them why they should choose you over the competition. I talked about this in the "Message Market Media" chapter.

You should also, of course, have a web-form on each of the pages of your website or, at a minimum, on the "Contact Us" page. This is so that if they're not in the modality to pick up a phone, they can simply type in their name, email address, and phone number and let you contact them. Again, make sure that you've got your phone number on the top right-hand corner. You've got a clear call to action telling them what to do next on every page of your website, under every block of text.

Check out our reviews, download a coupon, book an appointment. Explain why they should choose you. Leverage personality. Be authentic. Integrate your photos into your website. It really, really helps with conversion. Utilize your reviews, testimonials and videos. There's no reason you can't create a simple video for each of the pages on your website, explaining what the service is, and why your business can do it best.

Some people are visual, they can see the content on the website, read it and feel fine. If you can spend the time to provide both text and video, it really helps with conversion. Give them external proof. Take them out to the review sites where they can preview testimonials on Google Maps, Yelp, etc.

Show them what other people are saying, and you're going to significantly improve your conversion.

Chapter 8

Mobile Optimization - How to optimize your website for mobile visitors

More and more of your patients are searching for practices via mobile device. Here are just a few eye opening mobile stats that you should be aware of:

1. **50%** of mobile phone consumers frequent a retail outlet **inside 24 hours** of a local search on mobile (Marketing Land)
2. **50%** of mobile search is aimed at local businesses (Search Engine Watch)
3. **70%** of smart phone patients (and 77% of tablet consumers) believe the "**call button**" (or one click calling) to be critical on a mobile website (Clients Calling)
4. Approximately **70%** of mobile patients clicked the call button to call businesses directly from Google ads (this is a HUGE mobile search stat for you Adwords users)

5. 61% of mobile searches result in a phone call (because they're addressed at local businesses, like yours) (Dialog Tech)
6. **Over 50%** of mobile consumers are in the process of researching a purchase, or seek to make a purchase when they call a business directly (Local Vox)
7. More than half of all search volume results from smart phones, according to Google mobile search stats
8. Google reports that **40% of mobile consumers** turned to a competitor's web site after an unsatisfactory mobile Web experience, and **57%** wouldn't recommend a business with a bad mobile website.

Mobile smartphones can access websites, as well as perform a multitude of other tasks, which is why they have become more of a necessity than a luxury these days. For you, as a practice owner, this provides a unique opportunity to connect with local patients via their mobile devices.

Before you start to develop a mobile arsenal to drive more inbound calls, you must first figure out who your mobile competitors are. It is important to know who you are up against in mobile marketing so you can plan your strategies accordingly.

To effectively do this, you need to identify your closest competitors and learn what mobile techniques they are using to generate their sales.

First, find out which of your competitors have a mobile-optimized website. One quick and easy way to find out is to pull up their website on your mobile phone.

Did it load quickly? Was it easy to find their contact information and other details that consumers tend to look for while on-the-go? If so, they have invested in their business by making sure their mobile patients and prospects are taken care of.

Now, pull up your website on your mobile phone. If it's a nightmare, it's not your phone that is the problem, it's your website. This means you have been losing potential business.

Next, figure out which of your competitors are using text message marketing. If your competitors are doing it, they are probably telling the world to "text 123 to example." If you see promotions such as this, they are using text messaging to build a list of repeat patients.

This is one of the most cost-effective and results-oriented forms of marketing today. Text message marketing allows your competition to draw in local consumers with a great offer. Then, they send out occasional messages or coupon offers to keep them coming back to use their services.

Let's say one of your patients had plans to contact your business today after work, but they recently joined your closest competitors mobile list and had received a text coupon offer from them before they had the chance... Who do you think the patient will call?

There are many other forms of mobile marketing your competitors could be using to capture the attention of local consumers such as mobile SEO, QR codes and mobile apps.

If they are using these methods, it may be in your best interest to start researching how your business can do it even better.

Analyze Your Current Mobile Marketing Status

What is your status when it comes to staying connected with local consumers using Mobile Marketing strategies?

Researching your competition is a necessary task if your goal is to become the local authority in your niche. But, it is equally important for you to analyze where your business currently stands in order to move forward.

Are you currently running a mobile marketing campaign, but not seeing the results you want? Or, do you want to start a mobile marketing campaign but keep putting it off because you don't know where to begin?

Every business in your local area is in a crucial fight for more patients and profits. Therefore, in order to enjoy a spike in sales, your company can no longer ignore the profitability of ramping up your mobile efforts.

Many business owners pump a lot of muscle in competing with similar businesses, while neglecting to take a close look at what they're doing. Analyzing your mobile status will help you figure out which weaknesses are holding you back and which strong points can help you win the war.

You need to understand where your past efforts have taken you, as well as what your future has in store for you based on where you stand today.

For starters, it is crucial that you take note of what you are and aren't doing to generate more sales using mobile marketing.

Is your mobile website user-friendly? Does it load within seconds or take forever to render properly?

Does your mobile website have all of the relevant information on it that consumers look for while on the go?

Does your mobile website come up high in the rankings on mobile search engines, or is it nowhere to be found when local consumers perform a search for you "hearing aids + your city" or "audiologist + your city" on their mobile devices?

Have you started to build a text marketing list? If so, what are you currently doing with that list? Are you focused on building a trusting relationship or are you spamming them with offers on a daily basis and getting high rates of opt-outs?

Is your opt-in/call-to-action on all of your printed and web marketing materials?

Are you using QR codes as an additional method of increasing awareness about your business? Do you have your QR codes on all of your other marketing materials? Are you using them to direct traffic to your mobile website?

As you can see, there are a lot of things to consider when it comes to making sure your business is on the right track toward beating your local competition with mobile marketing.

Spy on Your Mobile Marketing Competitors

Do you want to know how your closest competitors are driving more business by using mobile marketing? Just take a look at their campaign yourself.

Mobile marketing has recently opened new doors for businesses that want to market their products and services by using mobile phones as personal mini-billboards. This has been enhanced by the fact that more and more people own mobile devices, and use them to find local products, services and businesses regularly.

To beat your competitors in the world of mobile marketing, you need to know what they are doing to be ahead of the curve. Digital technology is growing at astonishing rates and is not expected to slow down anytime soon. This alone is causing many companies to be left behind when it comes to new-age technology.

Spying on your competitors' mobile marketing initiatives may seem like a daunting task, but it's not. In fact, all you need to do is identify which are taking most of your patients and let the research begin.

You should begin by visiting their mobile websites on your phone. Go through the websites and take note of the look and feel, the features and the traffic flow. Although your goal is NOT to copy exactly what they're doing, you could get a few pointers for your own mobile website.

Next, find out how their text message marketing campaigns operate simply by joining their mobile list. They probably have a text call-to-action placed everywhere, so opt-in and pay close attention to what happens throughout the entire process. This is the perfect way to get a first-hand look at their services, products, and promotions.

Are your competitors using QR codes to generate interest in their business? If so, whip out your mobile phone and scan their codes to see what lies behind them. Where do the QR codes take you? What type of incentives are they offering to get people to scan them?

Another thing you can look into is your competitors' mobile applications. Download their apps and see what they're offering and how user-friendly they are.

The information you gain from your research should be used solely to set up your mobile marketing campaign that will not only beat your competitors, but will also attract new patients and keep them loyal to your business.

Spying on your competitors is not illegal, but there are limits you should follow to remain fair. Under no circumstances should you use unethical measures to jeopardize your competition in your quest for mobile marketing.

Make Patients Call your Practice with Mobile Marketing

The secret to beating your competitors in the business is making your company more interesting to your target audience. There are several ways to do this using mobile marketing if you plan ahead, focus on the right things, and maintain your campaigns over time.

As much as you would like to boot your local competitors out of the picture, the fact is that a lot of them will probably be using some of the same mobile marketing methods as you are.

So, your main focus should be geared toward making your patients choose your business over theirs. This is fairly easy to do if your efforts are consistent and persistent.

It is up to you which tools you use to work positively toward attracting new patients and keeping the ones you already have.

Here are a few tips that can work in your favor and help local consumers choose you:

- You need to have a good website that is mobile-friendly and easily accessible by mobile phone users in your area. People are using their mobile phones to access the web to search for local products and services while on the go. Make sure your site loads quickly, gives them the exact information they need, and is easy to navigate.

- If you choose to start a text message marketing campaign, make sure your text messages offer great value, relay a clear message, and are short and informative. Also, be sure to send messages out consistently, yet conservatively. Create a careful balance that makes sense for your business and your target audience. Need a boost in getting new mobile subscribers? Give your patients and prospects a great incentive in exchange for opting-in and watch your list grow exponentially.

- Consumers love businesses who stay "on top" of the digital age. They expect you to have a website, to actively involved in their favorite social media outlets, and to be easily accessible from their mobile devices. Have a mobile app developed to aid in keeping your local consumers connected with your business. Implement the use of QR codes as a way to keep your local consumers engaged and provide them with "instant gratification."

- Mobile SEO should be used effectively to attract qualified traffic to your website. Mobile users search for local products and services constantly on their mobile devices when on-the-go. If your business does not rank in the results, there is major potential profit leak left for your competitors to scoop up.

If somebody goes online, searches for your services, and gets to your website, they probably want to just get the basic information.

They probably are not interested in learning a ton of information about you. They simply want to find who you are, where you're located, what your services are, and then press a button to call you. You should absolutely set up a mobile version of your site, don't overcomplicate it, and give the basic information.

Now that you have your website conversion fundamentals in order and have a proactive Mobile Marketing plan, you can start to think about other marketing.

Chapter 9

Online Reputation Management – How to ensure once someone finds you online, they know you are the practice they need

Getting found in the search engines is only half the battle. What does that mean? Think about the last time you did a search for a local business or service on your mobile device or computer. What happened? You typed in what you were looking for a whole list of results showed up. Right?

Did you immediately look at the first result and call them without clicking into their website or taking a look at the reviews on their Google My Business profile? I would guess not.

This is exactly why your business needs to have an online reputation management process in place. If what sets your practice apart from the others is the attention you give to your patients, getting that relayed onto your online profiles is crucial.

When people are researching who to do business with online, they are associating your reviews with how good you are as a business. If you have no reviews, you will most likely get looked over right away due to the fact that your competitors in the search results are showing positive reviews on their profiles.

Let's say you have 1 or 2 random reviews on your profile from years ago and your biggest competitor has 10 reviews on their profile with a 4.9 overall rating, who do you think will win the business and get the first chance at that patient?

Humans are creatures of habit and we just want to go where everyone else is going. Fear of missing out is a real thing and extremely present in the online world. Use this to you advantage and start generating reviews for your practice today. Here is how:

Step 1: Start with Google. Google is the major search engine in the game and you will gain more from starting here. Make a list of 10 people you know who would be willing to leave you a review. These could be your best patients, family, friends etc. Text, Call or email these people and ask them to leave you a review this week.

This will give you a solid base to work with. It also provides you with some protection. Your business listing will not be a susceptible to a bad review if you already have 10 good reviews. This off sets the algorithm and how much 1 bad review can lower your rating.

For example, if you only have 1 review on your profile and it's a 5 star review and a upset patient comes along and leaves a 1 star review, your rating will now be a 3 star overall.

But if you have 10 – 5 star reviews and that patient comes along the same way and leaves a 1 star, you will still have a 4.5+ rating. The damage has been minimized.

Step 2: Claim all listings around the web that allow reviews to be left on them. For example: Yelp, Merchant Circle, Yellow Pages etc. Do a quick Google search for your practice name and claim all the profiles and directories that show up.

Step 3: Get some review management software in place. This will allow you to start monitoring all these sites around the web in one convenient dashboard. There are plenty of cost efficient options and a simple Google search will provide these.

With this software in place, you can set it to alert you anytime someone leaves a review on any of your profiles. This way you can quickly address it and not over look it.

Step 4: Start generating reviews on the other 2 platforms that require attention. Those are Yelp and Facebook. The reason I mention these is for a few reasons.

First, there are billions of users on Facebook and people have started using the review system on there as a way to figure out who they want to do business with.

Second, the next largest Search engine behind Google is Bing and they do not have their own built in review platform like Google. They pull Yelp reviews in and display those to users. This requires you to have a solid Yelp profile with at least 5-10 reviews on there, as well.

Third, both Facebook and Yelp review rating snippets show in the search results. What does this mean? See the image below.

> www.facebook.com › ... › Medical Supply Store
> **Lifetime Hearing Services, Inc. - Home | Facebook**
> **Lifetime Hearing Services**, Inc. - 522 W Palmetto St, Florence, SC 29501 - Rated 5 based on 25 Reviews "**Lifetime Hearing Services** serves the Pee Dee with...
> ★★★★★ Rating: 5 · 25 votes · Price range: $$$

> www.lifetimehearing.com
> **Lifetime Hearing | Technology and Care | Fort Worth, TX**
> **Lifetime Hearing services** the entire Fort Worth, Texas area, providing testing, hearing aid services, tinnitus treatment, and much more. Locations include ...

> www.healthyhearing.com › ... › Michigan › Marysville
> **Lifetime Hearing Services - Marysville, MI 48040**
> Read verified information and hearing aid patient reviews for **Lifetime Hearing Services**, 1273 Gratiot Blvd, Marysville, Michigan, 48040. Your trusted resource ...
> ★★★★★ Rating: 5 · 7 reviews

See how the star ratings for this Practice are showing in the search results? Now imagine if these we're the opposite and all 1 star. Anyone who searched for this practice would immediately look elsewhere.

Step 5: Work on driving 5-10 reviews per month to your listings with your review software. This requires a team effort and really getting everyone on board, but when done properly, it will give you a massive advantage over your competitors. If you have 100+ 5 star reviews on your Google My Business and the competitors all have less than 20, who do you think is going to win the majority of the business from online searches?

Step 6: Get started on this today! Don't wait!

Chapter 10

Social Media Marketing – How to leverage social media (FB, Twitter, Instagram and other platforms) for maximum effect in your practice

There is a lot of BUZZ around Social Media (Facebook, Twitter, Instagram, YouTube, LinkedIn), but how can it be leveraged by a Practice? How can you use social media to grow your practice?

In this chapter we are going to cover social media marketing for your practice. I hope that by now, you've learned a lot about how to position your company online, how to rank well on the organic listings on the Google Map, and how to rank well in the organic non paid listings. Now, we're going to talk about social media marketing, and how you can utilize social media tools like Facebook, Twitter, Instagram, and LinkedIn to grow your business.

As I talk to practice owners throughout the country about internet marketing and social media, I tend to get a puzzled look. The question is, "How in the world does all of this social media stuff apply to my business? How can I possibly use Facebook and Instagram in a way that would help me grow my revenues, grow my patients, and get more repeat business?"

I'd like to try and bridge the gap on where the lowest "hanging fruit" for social media is in your practice by asking, "What's your number one source of business today" Just stop and think, where does most of our revenue come from? You'll quickly come to the conclusion that your number one source of revenue is repeated and referral business.

The lifeblood of any service business is your existing patients returning for services over time, and your existing patients referring you to their friends and family. If social media is harnessed correctly, it gives you the ability to take that repeat and referral business, inject it with steroids, and take it to a whole new level.

Let me explain why I feel that it's a great place for you to really connect with your patients and get more repeat and referral business. Just a couple of Facebook stats:

Facebook currently has 2.41 billion users.
The average user has 338 friends, and checks in between 6 and 9 times per day.

If you can get your real patients, current and past, your sphere of influence, to connect with you on social media,

Facebook, Twitter and/or Instagram, your business is exposed to their 338 friends as soon as they "like" and follow your page.

It's almost as if they'd sent an email, or they'd sent a text message out to all their friends saying, " I use this great practice in our area. The next time you need their services, why don't you think about them?" It's extremely powerful to gain exposure to their sphere of influence.

Another major advantage is that they've given you permission to remain top-of-mind with them. The average user, like I said, checks in between 6 and 9 times per day. They login to check out the updates on their Facebook wall and to see the updates of all the companies and people they have liked or are friends with. If you're posting updates to your social media profiles, the people who have liked your page are going to see the new content whenever they login.

They are going to see an update and your logo. They're going to see some special offer or promotion, and it's going to peak their interest. Next time they need your services, who do you think they're going to call?

There is a higher probability for them to use you again, and refer you to their friends, because they remember you and had a good experience with. They know who you are. You've remained top-of-mind. If you look at major companies like Coca Cola, Pepsi, and Lay's, they spend billions of dollars a year on advertising and promotions; TV, radio, print. What's the whole thought process behind that? They're developing their brand, so they can maintain what we call "TOMA," top of mind awareness. Leveraging social media inside your existing sphere of influence is a great way to tap into that top-of-mind awareness.

Where should you start? Where can you start using social media, with all of the different platforms out there? With so many different social media tools, what should you be using?

- Facebook
- Instagram
- Twitter
- Linkedin

In chapter two, we talked about having a blog and putting out consistent updates. Well, blogging ties very nicely to your social media strategy. These are the social media profiles you definitely want to have set up and ready to roll in your business.

Let's talk strategy before we get into the granular details. Talk about high level. How do you leverage social media and how do you gain that initial following?

Well, first of all, you want to utilize email to get initial engagement. Having an active social media profile with daily updates is not worth anything if you don't have likes or viewers.

Now, at the same time, if you have thousands of irrelevant people that have pressed like on your website or on your Facebook profile, it's not going to work to your advantage if they're not people in your area. They're not the target market that we discussed in the marketing fundamentals.

You want to make sure that you have a strategy to get your real patients and your true service area engaged with you in social media. You should leverage email to engage your patients to get to your social media profiles. We take a multiple-step process.

The first thing you want to do is build that list or go into your practice management system, if you have one, and export the name and email addresses of your patients.

Grab current patients, past patients, sphere of influence of your friends, your business partners, people that you do business with, and put them into an email list.

Queue up a nice little message that says, "Hey, we appreciate your business. We appreciate your relationship over the years. We're getting active in social media and would love to have you engage with us. Please go to facebook.com," and give them a direct link to your Facebook page, "and press the like button."

There are a couple of things you can do. You can offer them an incentive, something of value like a coupon or a discount. Or, if you feel like you've got an active patient base that knows who you are and likes you, just ask them to do it as a favor.

You'll be able to start building that following. Now, you don't want to stop there. You don't want to just send one email out that says, "We're on social media." You now want to build it as part of your business.

In the Google Maps Optimization chapter, I talked about having an email go out after thanking the patient for their business and asking them to go ahead and write a review for you on one of the various online directory sites.

Well, there's no reason you couldn't send a subsequent email to that contact, maybe a day or two days later, that says, "By the way, we're actively involved in social media and would love it if you would engage with us." Then give them a direct link to your social media profiles where they can press like, subscribe, and follow to start engaging with you on social media.

The key is that it needs to be an automated process where you're typing your patient's name and their email address. These emails go out to everybody that you serve without any hiccups, without any potential for dropping the ball. If you don't do it consistently, you won't get a true following and you won't get your real patients engaging with you on these social media platforms.

That's step one. Leverage email to build that initial engagement and that following of your real patients. Remember, we want authentic patients, and not just throwaway links and subscribers.

Once you've got that part squared away, you have got to think about what are you going to post. What information are you going to put up and how frequently? You should post to your social media profiles fairly often but do not over due it.

These should be informative posts. It should not be a sales pitch. It should not be, "Here's 10-percent off your next purchase."

You can do that every now and then but more than 80% of the time it should just be social content: "Here's a tour of our practice", "Meet Our Team" etc.

Keep it informational, keep it relevant, keep it social, and then you have to engage. Social media isn't a one-way dialogue. You shouldn't be going to your social media profiles and pushing out updates that don't have any engagement. You shouldn't just be posting. You should be trying to get people to reply to your post: "Hey, that was funny", or "That's a beautiful picture", or "Thanks for that great tip," all of which you can reply back to.

Then, listen to what your fans are saying. Once you've got a flow – you've got 50, 70, 100 or a couple of thousand people that have liked you – you are going to be able to hear what they are saying as well. They might post something that's totally irrelevant to you, like "Hey, tomorrow's Billy's birthday." There is no reason that your organization couldn't reach out and say, "Hey, wish Billy a happy birthday for us!", from your company. They will think, "Wow, this is a company that cares. This is a company that's real and authentic."

Engaging in social media is probably the lost art. Most people that use social media just post one-way messages, which is not the idea. It's a social platform, so there should be conversation. There should be dialogue.

The next thing you want to do is to develop your brand and make sure that you enhance the bio section on each one of these profiles. Within Facebook, Twitter, LinkedIn and Instagram, you will have the option to fill in an 'About Us' or bio section. Write some interesting information about your business there.

Take the information from the 'About Us' page on your website where you talk about where you guys were founded, why you started the business, the service that you offer, etc. and pop that into the bio section on your social media profiles.

You also have the ability to put an icon on each one of these social profiles, and you want to make sure that you're using an image that represents your business. It can either be a shot of the practice, the team or it can be a logo.

People tend to buy from individuals more than they buy from businesses because a business is an anonymous entity and a person is someone that they feel they can get to know, like and trust.

It's all about branding, so make sure that you're leveraging the header graphic and the image icon. If there is an option for you to customize the background, do it! You want to make sure that you've got the elements that marry up with the overall branding of your business.

Make sure everything on your social media profiles is consistent with your website. On your website, you've got a color scheme, a logo, and maybe you've got brochures that are made up. Make sure that there's a consistent flow, look, feel, and color scheme on all of your social media profiles, website and offline materials.

Don't forget to have a plan; how often are we going to post? What types of posts are we going to put out there? How are we going to engage our patients? What social media profiles are we going to be involved with? Remember in chapter two we talked about the fundamentals of your marketing plan (market, message & media). You need to make sure that you have a clear understanding of who your patient is and who your ideal patient is. Then, make sure that you are crafting a message that will resonate with that particular patient. You need to think about all of these things as part of your social media strategy.

Don't just dive in. A common mistake would be to just setup the profile and start posting with no thought process or plan behind it. Think about it. What pages are you going to be on? What message are you going to put out? What color scheme are you going to use? Set all of that up and then get very specific about who your target is.

One solid method is to schedule your post types:

Monday, Wednesday and Friday are the days that you are going to put up tips; Ex. Hearing aid care tips, etc.

Tuesday and Thursday, you'll post photos; pictures of really interesting things relative to your business; pictures that are interactive.

Saturday and Sunday you post coupons or offers.

I am not saying this is the editorial calendar you should follow. However, the point is to make it easy for yourself so that you know what is going up and when. You can be streamlined and it can be automated.

When we talked about the blog in the SEO chapter, we went over leveraging content. Because that content is king, you have to be creating updated information on a consistent basis. This content can go up in various places. As you post a new piece of content, it can go to your Facebook, Instagram and Twitter pages automatically. If it has a photo included, and you can take your blog content and syndicate it to recreate great social media content.

Remember, content isn't necessarily just written text. You are an expert on your craft. You know things that the average consumer doesn't. Utilize and share that knowledge.

You can either sit down and write about it, you can take an audio recorder and record yourself talking about it, or if you're comfortable on video, you can break out the camera phone and shoot a video talking about an issue that your ideal consumer may be facing.

One video post can result in several forms of content.

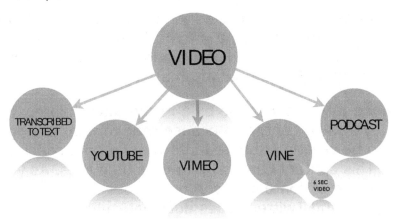

That one piece of content can serve multiple functions. The first function can be posting videos up on the social media, on websites like YouTube, Vimeo, and Wisita, where you can upload interesting clips and videos.

You can also take that video and have it transcribed using a service like castingwords.com. There are various transcription services. That video of you talking about the benefits of flu shots can now be transcribed into text, which may then be used as a blog post and be syndicated into your social media profiles. Another step beyond that is using that same audio and turning it into an audio podcast that you can have hosted on your website.

There are a lot of things you could do, to take your content and work with the modality that you're most comfortable with. Some people like to write. Some people like to talk. Some people like to be on video. Figure out what you are most comfortable with and run with that. This is how you create social media content for your online marketing plan.

Remember, educational content that's published in multiple places gives you industry expert status. This is going to drive your credibility, which in turn, will result in more referrals.

What not to post:

1. Use the 80/20 rule for marketing messages, put out 80% information and 20% marketing.

2. Keep it business related. Your political and religious beliefs are never a good mix with business.

3. Photos of your kids playing tee ball are good, but don't let it dominate your page.

4. Keep your vacation photos on your personal social sites.

5. Keep your business opinions, beliefs, and interests to yourself.

Sometimes knowing what not to post is more important than knowing what to post, because the natural tendency is to go to these social media profiles, and just post promotional material. So, don't post a coupon every single time you log in. If you do that, everybody that liked or subscribed to your page will start to disappear before you know it. They'll stop subscribing, they'll unlike you, and they'll un-friend you.

You have to use the 80-20 rule for messaging: 80 percent informational and fun stuff, and only 20 percent should be promotional.

Try and keep it business related. You don't want to get into your political and religious beliefs, because if somebody disagrees with you, you can create a negative atmosphere. That's not something you want to do on your business profiles. You've got a personal profile for a reason. If you want to put your religious and political beliefs there, knock yourself out. Just keep it off of your business pages.

You may not necessarily want to put too many photos of your kids on your page, even though if you're a personality brand. Don't let your kids and your family be the dominant positioning behind your business profile page. Obviously, keep your vacation photos and again, your opinions and beliefs, off your business page. Family photos are another thing that should be kept primarily on your personal profile.

When and how to engage

We talked about asking your patients to 'like you' on Facebook, and asking your patients to write testimonials. We also talked about interaction and responding to your patient's actions. "Hey, thanks so much for the follow. We appreciate it." Or, if they write you a testimonial, make sure you blow that up.

Not only should you say thank you, but you should also share it. "Hey, Jean, thanks so much for the positive testimonial. We appreciate your feedback. We appreciate your business, and this is what keeps us going. This is what we're in this business for." Then, you could take that testimonial and put it on your website, or embed it on your website through the various widgets and short codes that Facebook provides.

This is just a way to put out relevant content, and if you're paying attention to your feed, you can turn it into some great conversation. Again, you want to be active on social media. It's a great way to get repeat or referral business. You need to be on Facebook, LinkedIn, Twitter, YouTube, and Instagram. You want to utilize email marketing to gain that initial following, and then post updates that are informative and not sales-oriented on a consistent basis, and engage.

If you do this regularly and correctly, you're going to grow a nice following of real patients in your true service area.

You're going to remain top-of-mind and it's going to help you grow your business in terms of the lifeblood of your organization, which is repeat and referral business.

Chapter 11

Video Marketing – How you can tap into the power of video online to enhance your visibility and drive better conversion

Did you know that YouTube is the 2nd most used search engine (ahead of Bing & Yahoo)? Most practices are so focused on search engine optimization, but neglect the opportunities that video and YouTube provide. Implementing a Video Marketing Strategy for your business can get you additional placement in the search results for your practice keywords, enhance the effectiveness of your SEO efforts and improve visitor conversion.

There are a number of reasons that you should engage in Video Marketing for your practice. The primary reason is that it's going to increase your exposure on the search engines, giving you more placeholders for the keywords that are most important to you. It's going to enhance your SEO effort by driving great visitors to your website and creating relevant links to your website, improving conversion. Once somebody gets to your website, if there is good video on the home page and the subpages, that is going to resonate deeper with your potential patients. It will help convert those visitors from just browsing around page to actually picking up the phone and calling your practice.

Again, YouTube is the second most used search engine that there is. Obviously, Google is number one. One would think that Bing and Yahoo would be the other major search engines, but that isn't the case.

There are significantly less videos than there are web pages on the Internet. So, creating relevant and quality video content for YouTube and other video sharing sites is a really huge opportunity. These videos will help you to connect with people and answer their questions when they're looking for information on what you do.

I talked about the fact that you can now show up in search engines with an image next to it, and you can obtain multiple placeholders on Google for the keywords that are most important to you.

Video helps with your overall SEO Effort

The other thing that we can accomplish with video is the enhancement of our SEO efforts. As covered in the SEO chapter, links are critical for ranking. By creating good video content, you have the ability to drive inbound links to your website from high level video sites like YouTube, Vimeo, and Wistia.

Again, you don't want to have just the generic Home, About Us, Our Services, Contact Us pages on your website. You want to have a page for each of your core services and products. Videos that link to those pages is going to help with that SEO effort. Also, you're going to find that video content on your website, and on the pages of your site, actually reduces your bounce rate and improves the visitors' time on site.

These are SEO factors. 'Bounce rate' refers to somebody getting to your page and clicking back immediately, or browsing away. Google understands those actions as the page not being relevant to that search.

If the majority of the people that get to your site click off and leave right away, your bounce rate is high, and Google is going to start to show you less prominently in their results. That's part of the Google algorithm. The other factor is the amount of time spent on the site. If somebody gets to your page, stays there for ten seconds, and then moves on, the visit might not get treated like a bounce, but Google is looking at the length on the site.

If you have a video and a visitor takes the time to watch it in its entirety, that's improving your website visit length statistics. Even if they only watch a couple seconds of the video, you have captured their attention long enough that Google is going to see that your site is relevant.

Don't get confused by the notion that having video on your page automatically improves your SEO. That's not necessarily the case. But, having people stay on your page longer and not bounce off does impact SEO.

People like to watch videos. It's very rare, that you're going to see a video on subpages, but you'll find that if you do have that video content on the delivery page or the compounding page, people will take a couple minutes to watch it. Even if it is just because it's unexpected and it's more interesting than text. People enjoy listening to someone explain the topic that they are researching.

Another benefit that we have talked about is the fact that video gives you more placement in search. It's going to give you better search engine optimization because you get the links from the video sites, you're improving your time on site, and reducing your bounce rate. The other benefit of video that is probably even more powerful than anything, is that it's going to improve conversion.

You can have the best SEO strategy in the world, by driving hundreds of people that are looking for your services to your home page or to your subpage on a daily basis. But, if it's not converting and if people aren't picking up the phone and calling or coming to your practice after they visit your site, you're missing a major opportunity.

One of the main things that having intelligent video on your site is going to do is that it's going to improve conversion. The fact is that video clips resonate with people. They like it because it gives them the chance to get to know and trust you before they call you, especially if you follow my strategy rather than creating a super corporate video. If you create authentic video of your team, the owner or your audiologist talking directly to the camera, connecting with you on an emotional level, answering questions and giving a strong call to action, your conversion rate will improve.

It also gives you the ability to connect with different modalities. Everybody thinks in a different way. Some people are readers and will read all of the content on a page. Some people are listeners, so if there's the opportunity to listen to something rather than read, they'll choose to listen.

Other people like something visual. By having video on your website, combined with text (I'm not saying to abandon text), you have the opportunity to connect with every type of person. Some people will watch the video and only connect with that, because they wouldn't take the time to read a plain text web page.

How can we leverage video? We understand that it's powerful, it's going to improve your SEO, it's going to help us get better placement on the search engines, and it could potentially help with conversion. How can we expand upon this?

What we want to do is create simple videos about your company, your services, and the most frequently asked questions. You are then going to upload those videos to YouTube and other video-sharing sites, and syndicate them to your website and social media profiles.

What type of video should you create? Like I keep saying, "People resonate with people." Keep it simple, be real and be personable. Put your real face on the camera, or the face of someone that represents your company. Be frank and to the point. It doesn't have to be a 20-minute video. An appropriate length would be 30 seconds to 3 minutes long, enough to get the message across.

Don't overthink it. Don't feel like you have to go all out and hire a high-end production crew, or go out and buy a HD camera in order to make this happen. The reality is, you can create video clips using technology that you already have. If you've got a smartphone or a webcam, you have the ability to create video content that will work for your website.

You don't need high-end editing software either. YouTube gives you the ability to upload regular video and edit it right within the system. By edit, I mean cropping and tailoring the video to begin and end where you wish. You can put your phone number down in the bottom area of the video as well as a link to your website. Or, you can use a simple editing software like iMovie (free with Macintosh computers) and Movie Maker (free with the PC).

Using the technology that you already have, stand in front of the practice or a sign with your logo, and talk to the camera; talk with the people that are visiting your website, because that's going to stick with them.

What kind of videos should you create? You can create just about anything you want. But, the ones that are going to be most relevant are the ones that pertain to your services.

The first video that I recommend you make is an introduction for your website. This can be as simple as, "Thank you so much for visiting the XYZ Practice website. We specialize in providing hearing care services to the XYZ area. These are the things that make us unique and why people tend to choose us. We'd love the opportunity to serve you. Give us a call right away at the number below, and we can help you today."

A simple video along those lines should be the first step of your plan. It's a necessity.

The other videos that you want to create should be about your primary services. This ties in well with the SEO strategy discussed previously. You want to make sure you have a page on your website for each one of the services that you provide.

So, you don't simply provide hearing aids. You've got other services you provide as well. Make a list of the services that you want to attract more business for and shoot a brief video about each.

The other very powerful piece of content that you should incorporate, but should be phase two, would be your frequently asked questions, or FAQ. Make a list of the questions that people tend to ask and create a little video about it.

This is common information to you, but the average consumer doesn't know. Creating a little video providing answers to these frequently asked questions makes for great video content for your YouTube channel, to be syndicated on your social media profiles, and/or uploaded to your blog on your website.

Now that we know what types of videos we want to create and how to create them, what should we say? Should we have a script? Should we wing it? You want to be natural, you want to be authentic, and you want to be real. Some people have to have a script because they don't feel comfortable doing video outside of a scripted methodology. But, if there is any way you can get in front of a camera and speak naturally like you would to a patient in person about your services, that's going to work best.

Here is a simple script you can follow: "At XYZ Practice, we provide a full range of hearing care services (to the specific area, whatever area you're in, or whatever service this video is about)." Have a brief description of what you do in that area, and then, "If you're in need of this service in your area, we can help. Call our practice today at 555-5555."

A simple video like that for each one of your services should always include the call-to-action telling them what to do. Also, if you feel comfortable with it, referencing a discount could go a long way.

Don't over think this. Think about the core services that you offer. Shoot a quick 30-second to one-and-a-half-minute video about each and you're ready to roll.

What to do with your video content

What are you going to do with the videos once you've got them? Now that you have completed shooting your videos, what you want to do is setup a YouTube channel.

You can do this by going to YouTube.com. You want to upload your video, name it correctly and intelligently, putting it in terms that somebody is going to search for it in.

If somebody is looking for hearing aids, they are going to type in "your city hearing aids." You want to name the video using your keywords.

When you upload it to YouTube, you want to title it "Denver Hearing Aids" or "Hearing Aid services" and then put a description with a link to your site. "Visit us online at yourcompany.com/hearingaids" and then include a description about what you do, briefly outlining what was said in your video.

Some YouTube best practices

When you setup your channel, make sure that you give it a "city plus service, name of your company" title, instead of just your company name. You are also going to add tags with keywords to it. Don't just leave the tag area blank.

Make sure you use your name, address and phone number in every description on your YouTube channel because this is a good citation source.

As covered in the Google Maps optimization chapter, citation development is critical (having your company name, address and phone number referenced consistently across the web). This is a great place to get citations. Also, make sure that there's an image avatar with your company logo. You can update the default image by putting in your logo or put a picture of the team or practice.

If you log into YouTube and create your channel, you'll get an email confirmation. Once you're set up, you can go to the "My Channel" settings and make some of the updates I referenced above.

To change your logo, simply click "change" and choose your image – a very simple step.

Where it says "Your company name," it's going to default to something basic such as your email address on Google. You can hit "change" and update it to say "your city practice" and then a dash and your company name.

This gives you the chance to get your YouTube channel itself to show up for your keywords in the search engine. You will also have the opportunity to add your channel keywords. That is where you can type in words such as "your city practice" and of course your company name.

From there, there's a section where you can click "About your company" and put a description about who you are, what you do, and what areas you serve. You can get as creative with this area as you want, but it is most important to make sure you first put a description of your services, and your city.

If you're in Tampa, you put Tampa. If you're in Lakeland, you put Lakeland. If you're in Los Angeles, you put Los Angeles. Put your phone number and, again, restate your name, address and phone number. Citations are important. Having this in the description area is powerful citation source.

Always put your name, address and phone number the same way as you did on your Google Map listing, your Yelp listing, etc. That way, you will be consistent across the web, improving the probability of ranking in the Google Map listings.

Now, let's talk about video tagging best practices. Let's say you created the inventory of videos I recommended: an intro video and clips for each of your services.

How did you tag those videos to maximize the opportunity and to make sure that you're going to rank well in search?

Title Video with City Service - Company (always mix this up a little)

- Description should always start with http://url.com and then describe the service using those same keywords. ALWAYS ADD N.A.P. INFO AT THE BOTTOM OF THE DESCRIPTION
- Use your keywords as tags and include the company name.
- Choose most appropriate screenshot
- Click "advanced settings" and add address to video

The first thing you want to do is have your primary keywords in the title of the video as well as a description that includes the "https://" before your web address.

In the description area, you can put in "We're a full service XYZ practice. We serve this area. This is our name, address and phone number," but at the very top, you should have your website address, including the "https://".

If you just put www.yourcompany.com, YouTube won't understand the link and it will show that it isn't clickable. If you put "https://" the link will be clickable, and visitors will go straight to your page, and they also get the link authority from having that link back to your website.

Choose the screenshot and add video. Whenever you upload your video you are able to control your title and your description, as well as the ability to add tags.

Again, don't call your videos "your company name." Don't call it "hearing ads." Call it "Your city + that service," and then your company name. Title your videos the same way that somebody would search.

If it's your intro video, you might want to call it "your city + your primary service" Ex. you're a local "Lakeland Hearing Clinc– Hearing Aids."

It is really critical that you have the right titles on your video. It is what is going to make it so that Google can locate it and include it in search results.

The next thing you want to do in your description is to put the link at the very top. The first thing you want to do is include a link back to the home page or to the specific page that you're discussing in the video.

If it's the hearing aid page, don't put a link to your home page. Put a link to that hearing aid page, and again "https://yourcompany.com" -- make sure you've got that "https://".

Below, you add your tags. Within those tags you can put in your city practice and everything in between.

What else can you do with your videos?

Now that you've updated your video and you've properly optimized it, your title is correct, and your description is posted, how can we use these videos? Where are we going to leverage them? Well, to really get the benefits of that conversion component, we need those videos to be posted on our website and social profiles as well.

The best way to do this is to copy the "embed code" and post the videos right on your site. The intro video should be embedded on the home page and the service-specific videos should be posted on the appropriate subpages. The way we do this is right within our YouTube channel or YouTube account.

Go to the video manager and find the list of all of the videos that you have. Choose the video that you want to post on your website, and choose the share and embed option.

You will then be provided with this little piece of code. It goes from I-frame to I-frame. This is the specific code for that video. If you are updating your website on your own, copy and paste the code right into your website's HTML. If you have a detached web manager, send the code off to them with details on where you want it posted.

Once the code is embedded in your HTML, it will show up on the page itself. That's what we really want to do with these videos. And, of course we don't have to limit ourselves to YouTube. There are a lot of very well-known video sharing sites out there.

Chapter 12

Email Marketing – How to leverage email and SMS marketing for more repeat and referral business

Since email communication has existed, so has Email Marketing. Email Marketing is one of the oldest forms of advertising your business on the Internet. Although it gets a bad rap because of all the spam going around, it's still one of the most effective forms of marketing.

I am a big believer in email marketing. It's a powerful way to get instant traffic to your website and getting the telephone to ring; but there is a right way and a wrong way to use it.

Did you know the easiest patient to sell to is the patient you already have?

Every self-proclaimed marketing expert will tell you that that's nothing new. With that said, many business owners hardly ever market or keep in touch with their existing client base. Companies will spend thousands of dollars trying to get new patients but never think to ever into the clients who already buy from them.

Why is that? I have a lot of ideas about this. I suspect business owners think that once a patient buys from them, they will just keep coming back on their own. Or, maybe they simply don't want to bother their patients. The truth is, patients want to hear from you and they want to be touched by your business. If you don't, your competition will.

How do we start an Email Marketing campaign?
The first thing you need is an email marketing service. You shouldn't do this yourself for several reasons:

1. Your Internet Service Provider (ISP) will blacklist you for sending bulk mail.
2. You would have no stats for tracking your open emails
3. It would look unprofessional coming from your Microsoft Outlook box

With that said, lets take a look at some of the popular email marketing services, all of which are paid services and are priced based on the amount of emails you send. They all start at around $15.00 per month to send a couple hundred emails.

Constant Contact
I have used Constant Contact in the past and I like it for several reasons. It has great tracking stats, the ability to post to your social networks and a pretty user friendly interface.

Constant Contact has many templates available for use. Or, you can add your own custom templates. I think custom templates are a MUST for any business wanting to promote their brand. You will have to know a bit of HTML but if you don't, you can have a web designer create one for you at a fairly inexpensive cost.

MailChimp
Mailchimp is another service I have personally used and recommend. It's fairly easy to use and offers similar features to Constant Contact. The interface is clean and easy to use. You can use this for free if you have less than 2000 contacts.

I think borh of these services are a good solution for the practice looking to add email marketing to their internet marketing strategy.

How to get email addresses
I am asked on a regular basis about how to get email addresses. It's really not as easy as sending a letter in the USPS mail to anyone you want to. The reality of it is that just because they are your patients and you have their email address, doesn't mean you can send them anything if you don't have their permission.

This certainly is a fine line, because you somehow already have their email address, and they have used your services before, so is it really considered spam? Technically, yes. You didn't ask them if you could send them specials or a newsletter in email form.

The first thing you really want to do is get your clients' permission to add them to your email list. There are a variety of ways to do this, including placing a form on your website, putting a sign-up sheet on your counter or even a putting a spot on your receipts.

Explain that you send out tips about your industry or specials on a monthly basis, and would love to have them on your mailing list. You might even offer a discount coupon off your services if they sign up.

Getting that email address is valuable, so if it cost you 5%, go for it. Remember, you want the opportunity to have your company's name in front of your patients every single month. You want to remain top-of-mind if one of their friends are looking for services like yours.

Start building your list today.

What to send and how often

First, what do I send? You must use the 80/20 rule, 80 percent good information and 20 percent sales. If all you send is emails about what services you offer, no one will ever read it. It's a great way to kill your list.

Draft up some information about your industry, give good tips, and make sure it's information that will help your users. For the 20% sales, add a coupon or a special you are having, or offer something for your patients' friends and family.

How often you send your emails is very important. I always go with once per month, around the same time every month. It is important to commit to a date. More than once a month is too much and annoys people. I get an email from a company I purchased from in the past and get 3-4 emails a week from them, 100% sales, sometimes several times a day. I HATE IT and it drives me nuts. I removed myself from that list very quickly as I'm sure others have as well.

Get Legal
Make sure you allow patients the option to Opt Out of receiving email messages at the bottom of every message. Make sure that it's easy because nothing is more annoying than receiving emails that you don't want. If someone does

not want to receive your messages, then remove them from your list. They may be getting emails from too many sources and just want to clean out their email box. It does not mean they will never buy from you again. But I will tell you this, if they want out and you keep sending email to them, it's a sure-fire way to bother them and they will likely never buy from you again.

Again, you want to leverage email marketing as part of your overall internet marketing strategy. The best way to use it is to be sure you're collecting the email address from all of your patients and prospects. From there, use email marketing to get online reviews, engagement on your social media accounts and remain top-of-mind as a strategy to get more repeat and referral business.

Chapter 13

Pay Per Click – How Google Adwords, Facebook, Instagram and other social media platform ads can drive a flood of new patients to your practice every month

In this chapter, we're going to talk about Pay-Per-Click Marketing to help you understand how it works, why it should be integrated into your overall strategy, and how you can run a really effective program that can drive nice, profitable business for you and your company.

Why PPC should be part of your overall online marketing strategy

- Start showing up quickly
- Show up as often as possible where your patients are looking

- Show up for non geo-modified terms, such as "audiologist", "hearing aids" etc.

First of all, PPC gets things happening quickly, unlike an SEO program, setting up your website, building links and having the right on-page optimization. That process takes a little bit of time to materialize. What you do today and tomorrow, will start to pay dividends in three to four months.

With PPC advertising, you set up your campaign and will start to see your ads serve in just a few days. It can drive good traffic, especially during the times when you need to make sure you're visible.

You want to show up as often as possible when someone's looking for your services. Having a pay-per-click ad that shows up somewhere in the top, on the map, and in the organic section is important. Now you've got the opportunity to show up multiple places and significantly improve the chances of getting your ad clicked on, as opposed to your competition. A pay-per-click campaign gives you that additional placeholder on the search engines on page one.

It also gives you the opportunity to show up for words that you're not going to show up for in your organic SEO efforts. This is what I like to call non-geo-modified keywords. SEO and our whole organic strategy gives us the ability to show up in search engines when someone types in your city service, your city practice, your city audiologist, etc. All of those include some kind of geo-modifier (your city). They're going to put their city or their sub-city in that search for you to rank.

With a pay-per-click campaign, you can show up for the non-geo-modified terms (Ex. Audiologist, hearing aids, etc.), and put in the settings that you only want to show up for people within a 25-mile radius of your practice. If you're in Miami and somebody searches within that area for "audiologist" or "hearing aids," you can set it so that it only shows your ad for the people that are searching within that area. And Google can manage that through IP addresses by isolating where the search took place.

Google can also isolate who ran that search, where they ran that search from, and then place the ads based on the advertisers that are set up for that area. You only pay on a per-click basis, but you're able to show up for those keywords in those major markets. Another reason that you want to consider running a pay-per-click campaign is because you can run mobile PPC campaigns. With mobile PPC campaigns, when somebody is searching for your services from a mobile device, it's typically because they need immediate service. They're not as apt to browse multiple pages or listings. Now, if somebody runs a search on their mobile device, and you have a pay-per-click campaign set up, that search will be PPC enabled. They can simply hit your ad and, rather than browsing to your website and researching, automatically be calling your company.

On a pay-per-click campaign through mobile, you're actually paying per call as opposed to paying per lead. It's very powerful, and these are the reasons you want to have pay-per-click as part of your overall Internet marketing plan.

The Pay-Per-Click Networks

So what are the pay-per-click networks? There are two major networks that manage pay-per-click advertising across almost all of the major search engines There's Google AdWords, which is Google's pay-per-click program, and then there is Bing, which is through Microsoft Search.

These both have their own network behind them, so when you pay for an ad or pay-per-click campaign on Google's search network, you're gaining access to their network partners just like you would with Bing's network partners. There are a variety of reasons to consider a Bing Microsoft pay-per-click strategy.

Google is the dominant player with no serious competition. More than 80 percent of all searches happen on Google.com. So, if you had to choose, you would obviously you want to use Google. However, you do get an additional 20 percent by tapping into Bing and Yahoo! There are different networks but those two make up the majority of the search market. Running a pay-per-click campaign on both Google AdWords and Microsoft Bing search will allow you to show up in the majority of the search engines that somebody might be using.

Understanding the Google AdWords Auction Process

Let's review how Google AdWords works. In the simplest sense, you're paying on a per-click basis and you can choose your keywords (Ex. audiologist, hearing aids, etc.). As you pick those words, you bid and you pay on a per-click basis.

So, let's just say you're bidding on the keywords "San Antonio audiologist," and there are a lot of other practices in that city that want to rank for that keyword. If you say that you'll pay $2.00/click and your competitor says that they'll pay $5.00/click, they're going to be at the top. Assuming nobody else has placed a higher bid, $2.00 is going to be ranked second and $1.20 is going to follow. I am about to explain why that isn't 100% of the reality. The fact is that you pay on per-click basis and you are bidding against the competitors to determine how you're going to rank on your keyword.

It's an auction, just like eBay. People are bidding and whoever can offer the most money is going to have the strong position. With that foundational understanding, we can now explain why most pay-per-click campaigns fail. What tends to happen is a lot of pay-per-click campaigns are built on the notion that the highest bid wins. So, advertisers pick their keywords, throw up the highest bid per click and hope that everything turns out the way they want it.

Why Most Pay-Per-Click Campaigns Fail

- Setup only ONE ad group for all services (audiologist, hearing aids, etc.)
- Don't use specific text ads and landing pages for groups of keywords
- No strong call to action or OFFER on the landing page

Typically, you setup only one ad group for all services, whether it's practice, drug store, etc. You should have one ad group instead of different ad groups for each type of service. Also, there's no specific text ads and no landing pages for those ad groups and groups of keywords.

What you wind up with is the same landing page and the same text ad, whether your patient typed in "audiologist," "hearing aids," "tinnitus," or "cochlear implants" in the search engine. Whatever was typed into the search engine was likely very specific, and should match up to a very specific page, but that doesn't happen. It all goes to the home page. With this strategy, not only is your campaign going to convert poorly, but your cost-per-click is going to be higher. I will explain why later in this chapter.

The other reason why most pay-per-click campaigns fail is because there isn't a strong call-to-action on the landing page. So, you were just charged $5.00 or $9.00 to get a potential patient to your website and the page isn't even compelling because it does not have a strong call-to-action. It doesn't tell the consumer what to do next. If you factor these common reasons that pay-per-click campaigns tend to fail, you can better prepare yourself and set yourself up for success in the way that you execute your pay-per-click marketing.

Understanding the AdWords Auction Process

Let's talk about how the AdWords Auction process actually works. It's not as simple as the highest bidder winning. It's more complicated than that. The reality is, Google needs to feature the most relevant results because their endgame is to get people to keep using their search engine over the competition. This is how they can keep their traffic up.

They can keep their usage up and maintain that 80% market share, but can also run AdWords and make billions of dollars per year. Ultimately it all comes down to relevancy. The second they sacrifice relevancy for dollars, is the second they start to become less of a player in their market. So, they had to figure out a way to make their pay-per-click program grow around relevancy. And so that's why they established the quality score. They need to make sure that the person or company who has more relevancy gets a higher quality score and as result, can have a lower cost-per-click.

The way I like to explain it is, if I go to Google and I type in "BMW," obviously I am looking for a BMW dealer or for information about BMW. Mercedes could say, "That's our demographic also. If someone types in BMW, they're looking for a high-end vehicle. They are probably in the market to buy. Why don't I bid on the word BMW?" Of course they can. However, the person that searched BMW isn't looking for Mercedes. So Mercedes could say, "I"ll pay $25.00 for everybody that clicks on me when they search 'BMW'."

But, BMW might say, "That's my brand and I am going to compete for it, but I am not going to spend $25.00 for every click on my own brand. I'll pay a dollar for every click." Based on quality score, Google may decide to serve BMW because it's in the best interest of the person researching the brand, the consumer. It's also in the best interest of overall relevancy. That's how quality score works. Quality score is really driven by three core components

- Click Through Rate

- Relevance

- Quality of Landing Page

- Click Through Rate
- Relevance

- Quality of landing page.

As somebody conducts a search and your website shows up on the page in the pay-per-click section, Google is tracking what percentage of those people saw your ad and wound up clicking through. That's one of the primary metrics that they analyze. So, if your ad is relevant, if it speaks to the person's needs, and if it's compelling enough to them that they click through, Google just made more per-click. This will make them willing to give you a higher quality score because you've got better click-through rate.

Also, relevancy is a major factor. How relevant is your text ad to the keyword that was typed?

Ex. If they type in "hearing aids," and your text ad reads

> "We're a practice in the Dallas area,"

> vs.

> "We offer hearing aids here in the Dallas area. Click here to get started now."

Which do you think is more relevant to the patient? Google wants their search results to be as applicable as possible. They're looking at your click-thru rate, they are looking at the relevancy of your text ad to your keywords, and they are looking at the quality of your landing page.

If your landing page (the page that you drive people to) doesn't match up with what the person just clicked based on your text ad, or if that landing page doesn't have a strong call-to-action and the person quickly returns to the search engine, that signals to Google that you were not very relevant. This will result in a quality score reduction.

Better Quality Score = Lower Cost Per Click for Top Positions

By having a higher quality score you can bid lower and still achieve the top position. This is where you can actually win in the pay-per-click marketing game because a better quality score results in a lower cost-per-click for those who hold the top positions.

Again, if we just look at the reason most pay-per-click campaigns fail, it's because:

- You only set up one ad group
- You had the opportunity to create a separate ad group for each one of your core services, but you don't use a specific text ad that's going to compel someone to click and improve your click-through rate
- You don't have a strong call-to-action that matches up with what the consumer was looking for
- You're not going to have high click-through rate, relevancy, or an applicable landing page.

All of these issues result in a lower quality score.

You're going to wind up paying more per-click. PPC marketing is very competitive. If you're paying more per-click you're not going to be able to spend that much because you won't be getting enough calls to generate return on investment. The visual representation of this would be like setting up one AdWords campaign for each one of your services and landing people on your home page.

That is a recipe for disaster.

That's exactly what you don't want to do.

The Other Side of PPC – Facebook and Instagram

Having a strong Google Adwords campaign in place is great because that is what we call responsive advertising or marketing. People are actively searching for what you have to offer and using Google to do it.

The person is in a mode of needing your services and looking on the web to see whom they would want to use to solve their problem.

Social media platforms, such as Facebook and Instagram, have ad platforms, as well. But here is the key difference – people on these platforms are not actively searching for what you have to offer. That doesn't mean they won't be interested, it simply means they are not on the platform for research like they are on Google.

This means your ads need to be structured differently. The average person sees and hears anywhere between 3k and 5k different ads per day. That is everything including tv commercials, radio commercials, signs and billboards while driving and then what they see in the internet.

This means when you run Facebook and Instagram campaigns, your ads must be strong offers and straight to the point. You only have a few seconds of someone's attention and you need to capitalize on that with something they will want or need.

The Strategy

Crafting a strong strategy for these platforms will mean the difference in winning campaigns and losing campaigns. A solid strategy you can deploy would be to have 3-5 active campaigns going at all times. The first campaign should be a general ad used for branding purposes. Create this ad to let people know who you are, where you are and what you do. Do not get specific with the targeting. Keep the age demographics very wide, keep the radius at least 10-15 miles around your practice and do not add any specific demographics in the targeting section.

This will allow this ad to be seen by as many people as possible, which is what we want. You can use a picture of your practice as the image for the ad. Having people see this ad numerous times in their news feeds will help with brand recognition and top of mind awareness when they need something you can help them with. Let this ad run continuously – change the image every few months.

The other 3 or 4 campaigns will be offer specific. This means each ad will be centered around a specific offer or service you have. For example, lets say you want to do a campaign for cochlear implant services in your practice. Create a landing page on your website allowing people to sign up for a time to come in to the practice, sit down with someone and get more information. Then create an ad that targets people who would need this. This targeting will differ from the general ad because the age target will be 40-65+, the radius may be wider than the 20-25 miles we used in the general ad, etc.

Campaign Ideas

If you are looking for some campaign ideas and inspiration, here are a few you can use in your practice:

- Hearing Aids
- Tinnitus
- Financing Offers
- Trade In offers
- Meet the team
- Employee spotlights

Those are just few to help get the ideas flowing. Sit down with your team and brainstorm some more!

Chapter 14

Retargeting – How to increase the conversion rate of your website and ads around the web with retargeting

Have you ever purchased anything on Amazon? Who am I kidding of course you have. Every one has an Amazon Prime account these days! Have you ever put something in your shopping cart on Amazon only to get distracted and then not complete the purchase or save it for later? Then you see that same item in an ad on Facebook later that day...that is retargeting.

I get asked all the time from people how they do that and the simple answer is cookies. No, not chocolate chip or snicker doodle, we are talking about browser cookies. A small piece of code that is stored on your browser that remembers what site you were on and what you were shopping for or looking at.

The good news is you can do this for your practice. The technology is now widely available and accessible for small businesses! Retargeting increases your conversion rate by up to 70%! Yes you read that right! Platforms like Facebook and Instagram have adopted this technology in full force and it works extremely well.

The Strategy

Here is how you can implement retargeting for your practice and start increasing the number of conversions you have. First, you will need to set up a Facebook business manager account or use the one you already have from a previous chapter. Once you have your Facebook business manager and ad account set up, create a pixel. This is the snippet of code that will be placed on your website and we pages. Facebook will give you this code and you can then give it to your web developer to place on your website. Once the pixel is in place, now the real fun begins.

Start by thinking about which pages you would want to retarget visitors on your website and make a list. For instance, if you have a page on your website for your hearing aids and you want to retarget visitors on that website, we will create an ad to do so. Go into Facebook ads manager and set up an ad just like we did in the previous chapter except the difference with this one is that we will be using an audience for our targeting as opposed to the demographics.

When selecting the audience, you will choose your pixel from the drop down and then the exact URL of the specific page we will be retargeting. You can choose to send them back to the same page they were on that caused them to be retargeted but that is not how I typically do it. Since they have already seen that page and didn't convert on it for whatever reason, I don't want to send them back to the exact same thing. Instead, I create a new page with language that speaks to them more directly because now I know that the only people seeing this page are people who are on this retargeting list. I can phrase my copy more specifically or even offer them discounts or incentives if they take action now.

Visitors will feel like you are speaking to them directly and be more inclined to take the action you want them to take. This is what causes such high conversion rates on this technology.

Here are some pages to consider retargeting:

- Home page – retarget anyone that lands on your website
- Specific services pages – retarget the people who were looking at these services
- Book Appointment page – serves as a constant reminder for people to book the appointment
- Giveaways/Contests/Promotions – retarget anyone from these pages to make sure they take part

That should give you some ideas and inspiration on which pages you can retarget and how to effectively use this for your practice.

Chapter 15

Proximity Marketing – How to target your potential patients based on where they frequent, pull patients from the big box stores to your practice

At the time of writing this book, proximity marketing and geofencing are all everyone is talking about in the digital marketing world. But we see a lot of practices and agencies doing this wrong and not maximizing the full value and opportunity.

I want to dive into this and make sure you get a full understanding of what proximity marketing is, how it works and how to make it work for your practice. I am going to show you how to more or less, pull patients away from the big box hearing aid providers and have those patients come to you.

Let's dive in.

What is Proximity Marketing?

The simple answer is that it is marketing to people based on their proximity to a certain location. This means when they enter a specific radius to a location, they will start seeing your ads. This can also be called geofencing, which is a commonly used term.

When a location is chosen, a radius is then placed around the location and any mobile device that enters that radius can now be shown ads on different platforms such as apps. For example, a popular app that shows ads is the weather channel app. Every one checks the weather and usually has this app on their phone so it has become a common one used by businesses.

How Can You Use Proximity Marketing?

Now that you know what proximity marketing or geofencing is, you may be wondering how you can use it for your practice. The strategy we deploy involves making a list of 5-10 locations around your practice or city that would make good targets. Now, do not just pick high traffic locations because you think a lot or people will see the ads. That is not always the case. You want to think about places where people will be on their phone while they are in those locations other wise it is pointless to target that place. Places that may be good targets would be restaurants, movie theaters, doctors offices etc.

I mentioned earlier in this paragraph that you can use this technology to steal patients away from the big box stores and here is how you can do that. First, pick the 3-4 hearing aid stores near you that you would like to target such as Costco, Sams Club etc. Next, you put together some banner ads that will show to these patients going in and out of the practice. The messaging is up to you but we have found that pushing the "don't be just another number and come to the practice that knows your name" message works very well.

Now, a common question we get is "Won't the ads were showing in practices be useless after the person leaves the practice? Will they even see it while they are inside?" The answer is yes, but we do this a little bit differently for our clients and I am going to share that tactic with you now.

We utilize geofencing paired with retargeting. We have the ability to target a location and when a phone enters that location – it is logged into our software and our ads then follow that person around for as long as we want. This is huge when it comes to conversions because we don't lose that patient after they leave the practice that we had the target on.

The ads will then show on all their apps as well as their different devices. Meaning if they were on Facebook on their phone and saw the ad and then logged into their work computer, they would see the ads there too. Imagine how powerful that becomes when they keep seeing the same message across multiple devices and platforms.

Now that you know how proximity marketing works and how you can use it for you practice, what are you waiting for?

Chapter 16

Content Marketing – How to position your practice as the leader in your market

Content marketing or inbound marketing are two other buzzwords that get thrown around a lot in the marketing world, but for good reason. In this day and age, people are using the internet more than ever and that is not going any where anytime soon.

Patients are using the internet for research and looking for answers to their questions. Is your practice capitalizing on this and being the one to answer those questions?

If you are, great work and keep it up! If you are not, don't worry, its not too late to get started!

What is content or inbound marketing?

Content marketing is a marketing strategy based on creating and publishing content on the web for your target audience. Sounds pretty simple, right?

This includes everything from long form writing such as blog content all the way to video content you can post on youtube or your social media channels.

How to use content marketing in your practice

The common statement we hear is "I don't know what kind of content to put out!" Yes you do, you just don't realize it yet.

As a practice owner, practice manager or audiologist yourself, you are a subject matter expert. People come to you for answers about their hearing all day long, every day.

The key is to take those interactions and exchanges you have every day with patients and put that information online.

Are you hearing a lot of the same questions over and over? Those are perfect starting points! Grab your phone and film yourself answering those questions. Take that video and post it to you website and social media channels. That is content marketing!

Now, if you want to take it to the next level, here are some tips and tricks you can deploy.

Tip #1

First, make a plan to produce content every month no matter what. The key is consistency. This will get your potential patients used to the fact that you are putting out content on a regular schedule and it's something they can begin to expect.

When you are planning out your month, talk about what is relevant during that time of year.

Tip #2

Go check out a free website called answerthepublic.com. This is a website you can use to find out what people are searching for online. You simply type in a topic and the website spits out all the common questions people are searching for every month.

Tip #3

Have a call to action at the end of every piece of content you produce. If it's a blog article or a video, ask the person consuming the content to take some sort of action. Here is why: You have demonstrated that you are the expert and answered their question, they are now extremely likely to trust you and take you up on an offer.

Chapter 17

Track, Measure and Quantify – How to track your online marketing plan and ensure your investment is generating a strong ROI

Now that you've built and optimized your website, you've got an ongoing link building strategy in place where you're creating inbound links and moving up in the search engines, you have implemented email marketing and social media marketing initiatives, and have possibly implemented a paid online marketing campaign including Pay-Per-Click, you need to put some tools in place so that you can track, measure and quantify your data to ensure that you're moving in a positive direction.

There are a lot of different tracking mechanisms that you can put in place. I'm going to recommend three core tracking mechanisms. The first is Google Analytics. Google Analytics is a great website data analysis tool and it's completely free. Google Analytics will show you specifically:

- How many visitors got to your website on a daily, weekly, monthly, and annual basis.
- What key words they typed in to get there.
- What pages on your website they visited.
- How long they stayed.

The main thing you want to see from Google Analytics: when I started this whole Internet Marketing process, how many visitors was I getting to my website? Maybe it was 5, 20, 100, or 500, but it's good to know. Then you can compare to future data on an ongoing basis.

Ultimately, what you are looking for is whether or not the number of visitors to your website is increasing. Is the variety of keywords that they're finding you with increasing? Are you moving in a positive direction?

You can also set up reports within Google Analytics. To get set up on Google Analytics, you just go to Google.com/analytics. It's a simple process. You verify that you own the website through a variety of different methods, and then you install a small piece of code into your website's HTML. After you have done that, you've got the tracking in place and you're ready to go.

Keyword Tracking

The other tracking mechanism that I recommend is keyword tracking. At the beginning of this process, we talked about keyword research to determine what keywords people are typing in when they need your services. We came up with a list and all of those keywords were combined with your cities and sub-cities.

There are tools that will tell you how you're ranking on Google, Yahoo, and Bing for those various keywords. A few options include:

- Bright Local
- White Spark
- Raven Tools
- Agency Analytics

The keyword tracking tool I recommend is called BrightLocal. You can learn more about it at www.brightlocal.com. There is a cost associated with this service, but it is great resource for tracking your search engine optimization progress. You take your keywords, put them into the BrightLocal Keyword Tracker and then set up a weekly and monthly report that shows where you rank on Google, Yahoo and Bing for your most important keywords.

With a report like this, you can easily see how your website is trending in the search engines.

If you've built out the website correctly with the right on-page factors (title tags, H1 tags, meta descriptions, etc.), if you're building links, developing citations and have a proactive review acquisition system in place, you'll see yourself move up in the results. When you see yourself stagnating, you can go back to that keyword, figure out which page is optimized for it, look at your links and link profile, and whatever is necessary to push that keyword to the next level.

PPC Tracking

For tracking your pay per click (Facebook and Instagram Ads/ Adwords) efforts. I recommend Agency Analytics for this. There is a monthly cost associated with this one as well but the data you get is well worth it. You can track how well you campaigns are performing to prevent over spend on certain ads. Basically, when you have a winning campaign, you can increase that and when you have losing campaigns, you can kill those.

These are the types of tracking mechanisms I recommend. There are a lot of different things you can do, but having analytics, keyword tracking, and PPC tracking really gives you the most important key performance indicators to gauge your progress.

Next Steps

Throughout the course of this book, we have covered an abundance of information. We've mapped out your internet marketing plan and taken you step-by-step through how to claim and optimize your Google map listing, how to optimize your website for the most commonly searched keywords in your area and how to leverage social media to get more repeat and referral business. We then covered paid online marketing strategies like pay-per-click. If you have taken action and followed our instructions, you should be well on your way to dominating the search engines for the keywords in your area.

Need more help?

If you've gotten to this point and feel like you need some extra help to implement these ideas, we are here to support you. As experts in helping practices across the nation, we have had tremendous success implementing these strategies. You can call us directly at **866-237-5175** with any questions that you might have. Our team will review your entire online marketing effort (Website, Competition, Search Engine Placement, Social Media, etc.) and come back to you with a complete assessment of how you can improve and what you can do to take your online marketing efforts to the next level.

Request A Free Practice Acceleration Session Now.

Your custom acceleration session will:

- **Identify** key issues that could be harming your website without you even knowing it.

- **Look** at where your website stands compared to your competitors.

- **Determine** whether SEO is the appropriate route for you to take.

- **Uncover** hidden revenue that you're leaving on the table.

- **Offer** recommendations that you can put to use immediately.

Schedule your practice acceleration session now:
https://go.audiologyignite.com/schedule

About the Author

Shane Gebhards

Shane Gebhards is an entrepreneur, author, speaker and internet marketing consultant. He is the CEO of SVG Digital and Audiology Ignite. He has a passion for helping companies leverage best practices to increase sales, drive new streams of revenue and accomplish their goals. He's been involved in Web and Internet Marketing for over 12 years and started his own digital marketing agencies in 2013. Over the years, he has worked with hundreds of small and medium-sized businesses and developed strategies to help them grow their business by effectively marketing online via Search Engine Marketing (PPC), Search Engine Optimization (SEO), Social Media (Facebook, Twitter, LinkedIn) and other internet platforms.